A Louage

A History of Greek and Roman Classical Literature

A Louage

A History of Greek and Roman Classical Literature

ISBN/EAN: 9783744675871

Printed in Europe, USA, Canada, Australia, Japan

Cover: Foto ©Thomas Meinert / pixelio.de

More available books at **www.hansebooks.com**

A HISTORY

OF

GREEK AND ROMAN

CLASSICAL LITERATURE.

BY

REV. A. LOUAGE, C. S. C.,

PROFESSOR OF ANCIENT CLASSICAL LITERATURE AT NOTRE-DAME
UNIVERSITY, INDIANA.

NEW YORK:
D. APPLETON AND COMPANY,
549 AND 551 BROADWAY.
1873.

PREFACE.

HAVING to teach the class of ancient literature at the University of Notre-Dame, I in vain looked for a text-book for my pupils and for myself, and could not find any thing which would answer either my purpose, or the programme, such as I had conceived it. I found, among the books composing the classical department of the library, two volumes, in octavo, by R. W. Browne, on Greek and Roman classical literature. This work, which is deserving of much praise, was too extensive, and not systematic enough, in order to be given as a text-book. The "Classical Dictionary" of Anthon, and the one of Lempriere, both works of much erudition, would not answer my purpose either. I then set to work, and, taking the divisions of Browne, I collected information from the three writers named above, and also from some bibliographical articles found at the head of some editions of classical books, accepted as text-books in all the colleges of this country, and composed the present compendium, which I give as a " Manual," and which contains the history of ancient Greek and Roman classical literature.

The quality which I hope will be found in this work, and which, in my estimation, is the most important, is exactness. The indulgence of the reader is requested for many deficiencies in the style. Our main desire is to be useful, and to secure for our efforts the blessing of God.

S. N. D. B.

CONTENTS.

PART I.

GREEK CLASSICAL LITERATURE.

BOOK II.

SECOND PERIOD OF THE HISTORY OF THE CLASSICAL LITERATURE OF GREECE.

PART II.

ROMAN CLASSICAL LITERATURE.

BOOK I.

THE FIRST ERA.

CHAPTER I.—PROSE AND POETRY.

CHAPTER II.—DRAMATIC STYLE IN THE FIRST ERA.

CHAPTER III.—COMEDY.

CHAPTER IV.—SATIRIC DRAMA, SATIRE.

BOOK III.

THE SILVER AGE.

CHAPTER I.—POETRY.

CHAPTER II.—PROSE, HISTORY.

CHAPTER III.—PROSE, PHILOSOPHERS AND GRAMMARIANS.

APPENDIX.

PART I.

GREEK CLASSICAL LITERATURE.

PRELIMINARIES.

THE classical literature of Greece first engages attention because it is the oldest in Europe, and has been the source from which Rome derived its mental culture. Greece must be viewed in two different aspects: first, in its oneness as a nation; second, in its subdivisions into different races. In every thing which relates to Greece, we find a tendency to union, and an insurmountable principle of disunion and division of races. Each writer has common sympathies, but each one also exhibits in his productions the character of his race. Differences are found between the Ionians, Æolians, Dorians, and Sicilians. The Ionians show a refined and energetic mind, and reach perfection in every department of literature but the lyric. The Dorians and the Æolians show more disposition to enthusiasm, and among them poets are found who will win the crown in lyric poetry, and in the dithyrambic chorus; but perfection in the chorus has been attained only by the Attic or Ionian dramatists.

Greek literature has been imitated but not equalled. Greek literature is admirable, not only as presenting a picture of the human intellect in its highest state of perfection, but also for its moral value. Each writer writes not for personal glory, but in the discharge of a duty, in the performance of a mission—that of stirring the religious and national feelings of the Greeks.

The history of the classical literature of Greece should comprise only the history of the period when that literature reached its perfection, and consequently the period of the Pisistratidæ; but we will here consider also the period of the infancy of that literature, and divide this study into two books. In the first book we will examine the history of the infancy of the Greek literature, until the period of the Pisistratidæ, about 550 years B. c.; and, in the second book, we will consider the period which is called that of the Pisistratidæ, which extends itself until the supremacy of Macedon completes the destruction of the autonomy of Greece, about 300 years B. c.   -

Language being the material of literature, it will be necessary to say something about the formation of the Greek language.

Two families separated in the plains of Armenia: the Semitic occupied the south of Asia and the north of Africa; the Indo-European spread itself in the western part of Asia, and along the shores of the Black and Caspian Seas, penetrating into the northern part of Europe. To the Indo-European race we are indebted for the vocabulary and grammatical structure of the languages of civilized Europe; to the Semitic we owe the alphabet, and the means of committing ideas to writing. But while the Semitic race possessed, far earlier than the Indo-European, a phonetic alphabet of such power and perfection as to satisfy the requirements of both races, and to be capable of expressing and representing every sound, its comparative superiority ends here. The varied structure of the Indo-European languages, the power of combination in their elements, the perfection of their grammatical principles, endow them with greater capacity for forming a widely-diffused and extended literature.

In the Semitic languages the roots are few in number, and composed of only two or three letters, and the formation of words, by means of prefixes and affixes, is simple and in most cases similar; hence, although there are weight and dignity, there is an absence of that variety of sound, which, in the classical languages, falls so agreeably on the ear.

Doubtless the Greeks were distinguished by a vast amount of mental energy and subtlety of discrimination; but it is clear that the accommodating structure of the Indo-European languages was a powerful instrument to mould and educate their mental powers.

The ear, even of the uninitiated, is struck with the harmonious variety perceptible in the Greek language, and its fitness at once for the loftiest strains of heroic and dithyrambic poetry, the sweet pathos of the lyric muse, the rhythmical character of oratorical prose composition, and the simple familiarity and elegant perspicuity of narrative and conversation.

The Pelasgi were the tribes which settled earliest in Greece. They were allied to the Iranian tribes in the north of India, and consequently that element in the Greek language which exhibits an affinity for the Sanscrit, is the Pelasgic, and hence the numerous re-

semblances in words and inflections which are found
to exist between the two languages. The Hellenes,
who occupied, according to the testimony of several
writers, and especially of Herodotus, a portion of Thes-
saly, penetrated farther into Greece, and mixed themselves with the inhabitants of the country; and the
Hellenic element, being added to the other, caused the
older Pelasgian language to be looked upon as bar-
barous, when the Hellenes, who were an Ionian race,
became the possessors of Attica. This element of the
Greek language is said to have had an affinity to the
Persian.

The names given to the different tribes of Greece
have been differently explained; probably the way of
explaining their origin, by making them come from
the appellations of the chiefs, is not an accurate one.
We may find a more plausible explanation, drawing
them from circumstances of place, etc.: thus, the word
Dorian comes from Tor, or Taurus, which signifies
mountain. The Dorians were the inhabitants of the
mountainous districts; that race emigrated afterward
into Peloponnesus. The word Ionian comes from ʾΗιων
(shore). The Ionians settled along the sea-shore, and
the word Æolians comes from Αἰόλεις (mixture)—the
Æolian being composed of the Hellenic and Pelasgic
element.

Some authors pretend that the Semitic races had a
written language long before the Indo-European races,
and attribute to that circumstance the absence of literature, at least of poetry, among them. It might, with
as much plausibility, be attributed to the soft nature
of those people.

BOOK I.

CHAPTER I.

GREEK POETRY BEFORE HOMER.

Poetry is the earliest species of literature; it is the natural outpouring of the heart. Prose requires more intellectual development. In grief or joy we like to sing. The first verses were hymns to the divinity. Poetry, at the beginning, realized the definition of Strabo:

ʼΗ ποιητική πᾶσα ὑμνητική.

The first developments of Greek poetry were immediately connected with religion; and that worship, the enthusiastic devotion of which was embodied in poetry, was the worship of Nature. The Greeks were inhabiting a land well suited to nurture and foster the fancy and imagination.

The legend of Linus, which is found in the "Lamentations of the Bards," under the heading of "Αἰ Λίνε," symbolized the withering and perishing of Nature's life and vigor. Hesiod says of Linus:

Πάντες μεν θρηνοῦσιν ἐν εἰλαπίναις τε χοροῖς τε,
Ἀρχόμενοι δὲ Λίνον καὶ λήγοντες καλέουσι.

The other hymns were distinguished by the cry of joy, "ἰή Παιῆον." Poetry also sympathized with the joys and sorrows of domestic life, and it is clear what were the engrossing subjects of these strains; they must have been the praises of the gods, the melancholy legends interwoven with the popular mythology, the exploits of warriors and heroes, the joys of love and wine.

The names of the first bards and minstrels who occupied a high place in the respect and veneration of the people, are: Orpheus, Eumolpus, Thamyris, Musæus, Chrysothemis, Philammon, Olen, and some others. Their compositions are reported to have referred to the worship of Apollo, "the god of the sun." The first four were Thracians, and very likely had settled near Mount Helicon, and the names attributed to the Muses, or goddesses of song, owe their origin to the settlements inhabited by these bards, and other poets of that remote period.

The most celebrated of these poets is Orpheus, who sang the praises of Dionysus Zagræus (not Bacchus, the god of wine). The worship of this Dionysus Zagræus was of a pure character.

Those poets belong to the age of fable. It would be impossible to determine now whether the fragments which remain, and are attributed to them, come really from them, and even whether they ever existed or not. It is probable that Eumolpus, for instance, which means beautiful singer, owes his existence to family vanity.

CHAPTER II.

EPIC POETRY.

Homer.—Homer was born in Asia Minor, probably near Smyrna, on the banks of the Meles—hence the name of Melesigenes given to him—about nine centuries before the birth of our Lord. The authors cannot agree in regard to the time of his birth. Although seven towns claim the honor of being the birthplace

HOMER.

of Homer, we may hold our assertion as a good one, for, according to K. O. Müller, there is no such discrepancy in these traditions as at first sight appears. Smyrna was a colony of Athens, and it has been the mother city of Chios, Colophon, Salamis, Rhodes, and Argos.   The name of "Homer" (Ὅμηρος) means hostage, or, Ὁ μή ὁρῶν (the one not seeing).

Homer is the first who composed one of those wonderful works, an epic poem, of which few examples are found in the whole circle of the world's literature.

As far as we can ascertain, Homer travelled with Mentes, a Leucadian merchant, whose name the poet handed down to posterity in the "Odyssey;" he visited Greece, and the Greek colonies of Asia Minor, became the tutor of the children of Chiros, and died on the island of Irus, at a very old age.   On his way to Greece he landed, sick, on the island of Irus.   Some fishermen's boys asked him the riddle:

Ἆσσ' ἕλομεν, λιπόμεσθα, ἃ δ' οὐκ ἕλομεν, φερόμεσθα.

On this Suidas gravely remarks that he did not die of vexation because he could not guess the riddle, but of the disease under which he labored when he landed. He was buried on the island.   The inhabitants inscribed on his tomb the following elegy:

Ἐνθαδε τὴν ἱερὰν κεφαλὴν κατὰ γαῖα καλύπτει,
Ἀνδρῶν ἡρώων κοσμήτορα θεῖον Ὅμηρον.

Since his time it has been believed, always and everywhere, that he was the author of the two poems, the "Iliad" and the "Odyssey."   Only, at the time of the Ptolemies, some grammarians of the school of Alexandria pretended that Homer was not the author of the two poems, but that the "Iliad" and the "Odyssey" had been composed by different authors. The question was considered as a paradox, and gradually died away.

At the end of the seventeenth century, Hedelin and Perrault pretended that the two poems were the work of many poets, or bards, and that Homer was not the author thereof. Heyne accepted that opinion, and, in 1795, Wolf gave his "Prolegomena," by which he tried to establish the same theory. His arguments were the following: The two poems cannot be the work of Homer—1. Because they were not and could not be written; 2. Since they were recited, it is not probable that they were composed in longer portions than could have been recited on a single occasion.

We might concede that Homer did not write his poems, though it is doubtful (Nitzsch), and that concession does not solve the question against Homer. In regard to the second argument, we may say that the poems may have been committed to memory, and the custom of the Greeks' listening to six or seven tragedies on the same day, at the celebration of their festivals, shows that Homer might have given the whole of each poem upon any of those occasions.

In order to solve the question, we must study the work itself. Evidently these poems are the work of one man, if we find in them—1. General similarity of style; 2. Unity of plan; 3. Consistency in the characters. But such is the case; then Homer is the author of the two poems.

1. In both we find the Homeric verse, which is peculiar to that writer; the similes, the same dramatic power. The words are the same; the new words scattered in the "Odyssey" were needed; the changes in the finals come from the changes in the language, which may be accounted for by reason of the differ-

ence of time at which the two poems were written. The "Odyssey" is evidently posterior to the "Iliad."

2. The unity of plan is perfectly observed in both poems, as we may judge by the exposition of the argument of the "Iliad" in the following chapter.

CHAPTER III.

ARGUMENT OF THE "ILIAD."

THE poet proposes to sing of Achilles's wrath, and its terrible consequences to the Greeks. When the poem opens, more than eight years of the war are supposed to have passed away. Chryseis, who has been allotted to Agamemnon as his portion of the Theban spoils, is the daughter of a priest of Apollo; her father proposes to ransom her, but is refused. Apollo, in order to avenge the cause of his servant, afflicts the army with pestilence. Achilles calls a council, at which Agamemnon consents to restore Chryseis, but declares that he will take in her place Briseis, the favorite of Achilles. Hence a fierce quarrel arises between the heroes, and Achilles refuses to take part in the war. He then entreats Thetis to prevail on Zeus to avenge his wrongs; she accedes to this request of her son, and her prayer is granted.

Zeus, mindful of his promise to Thetis, deceives Agamemnon in a dream. A council of war is called, in which Thersites attacks Agamemnon for his conduct toward Achilles, and a battle is determined upon.

This furnishes an opportunity for enumerating the forces, both of the Greeks and the Trojans.

The armies now meet, and Paris challenges Menelaus; Helen is to be the prize of the victor. Menelaus is victorious, but Paris is rescued by Aphrodite, and conveyed to the apartments of Helen. Agamemnon then demands the fulfilment of the conditions.

Zeus sends Athene to renew hostilities, by causing some one to violate the truce. In the disguise of Laodocus she persuades Pandarus to shoot at Menelaus; he is wounded, and the battle begins.

The battle continues, and Diomede is the hero of it. Wounded at first by Pandarus, he afterward slays him. He pursues Aphrodite, and wounds her in the wrist; afterward he attacks Ares, whom he drives from the field.

As Athene is the patroness of the invincible warrior Diomede, Helenus sends Hector to Troy to advise a procession to the temple of the goddess. This gives him an opportunity of visiting Paris, and exhorting him to return to the field, and also of having an interview with his wife Andromache.

Another single combat is proposed, and this time Hector is the challenger. Ajax is selected by lot as the Greek champion. They fight, and, night coming on, the heralds separate them. A council is held at Troy, in which Antenor advises the surrender of Helen, but Paris will not consent. The Greeks fortify their camp.

Zeus forbids the gods to interfere, and, taking his seat on Ida, he weighs in a balance the fates of the two nations, and by his decree fortune favors the Trojans. They assault the Greek camp. Heré and Athene set off in disobedience to the divine command, but are stopped by a message from Zeus. Night puts an end to the assault, but Hector prepares for a renewal of it in the morning.

Agamemnon calls a council, and complains of the false promises of Zeus; in his despair he proposes to return to Greece. Nestor advises him to conciliate Achilles by restoring Briseis; some chiefs are sent to Achilles, but their proposals are treated with scorn.

Agamemnon cannot sleep, and resolves to seek counsel from Nestor and Menelaus. During that night Diomede and Ulysses go to the Trojan camp, slay Dolon and Rhesus, whose chariot and horses they capture.

Morning breaks, and Discord excites the Greeks to battle. Atrides distinguishes himself; Diomede, Ulysses, and Machaon, are wounded and leave the field. Achilles then sends Patroclus to inquire who is wounded. Nestor urges him to induce Achilles to return, or, if not, to send him, Patroclus disguised in his own armor.

The evil fortune of the Greeks still continues. Hector enters the camp, and the Greeks fly to their ships.

Poseidon sides with the Greeks, but Zeus continues to support the Trojans. Many heroes are slain. Hector leads the assault, upbraids Paris with his effeminacy, and hurls defiance at Ajax.

Nestor goes to see the bloody field; there he meets Agamemnon, who rebukes him for forsaking the field. Heré borrows Aphrodite's cestus, and, vanquished by love, Zeus sleeps. During that time Poseidon helps the Greeks.

The Greeks rally and rout the Trojans. Zeus awakes, reproaches Heré, and sends Iris to warn Poseidon from the field of battle. He declares that the Greeks shall suffer until the wrath of Achilles is appeased. Apollo then puts the Greeks to flight. Hector tries to burn their fleet, but Ajax saves it.

Achilles gives his armor to Patroclus, and sends him to the field. The Trojans, being deceived, fly. Patroclus pursues them, and performs wonderful feats of valor. At length Apollo smites him on the back, his head grows dizzy, his armor falls from him, and he is killed by Hector. On dying, Patroclus foretells Hector's death.

Menelaus defends the body of Patroclus; Hector takes his arms and puts them on. Zeus declares that he shall never return in them to Troy. Zeus now relents, and sends Athene to assist the Greeks. Menelaus apprises Achilles of the death of Patroclus, and bears the body from the field.

The groans of Achilles, at his friend's death, alarm Thetis. She comforts him, and furnishes him with a new suit of armor. He goes to the fight, and, at his very shout, confusion seizes the Trojans. They think of retiring to Troy, but Hector refuses. Achilles's new shield is described. Reconciliation between Agamemnon and Achilles unconditional. Achilles goes to battle.

Zeus permits the gods to engage in the battle. Æneas meets Achilles, and is saved by Poseidon, and afterward Hector is saved by Apollo. Achilles sacrifices twelve prisoners to the manes of Patroclus. The deities on both sides engage in the hottest of the battle.

Priam urges Hector to retire, but he refuses, and is killed; stripped of his armor.

The funeral rites are performed in honor of Patroclus, and games are celebrated.

Achilles still wreaks his vengeance on the corpse of Hector. The aged Priam begs his son's body, and Achilles, by the advice of Thetis, accepts the ransom. The funeral of Hector concludes the poem.

The same unity is found in the "Odyssey."

Some have supposed that there was an interpolation at the end of each poem. In the "Iliad," the subject being the wrath of Achilles, it seems natural that the poem should be finished as soon as that wrath has been pacified; but the episode of Priam asking for the corpse of his son is natural, and adds to the beauty of the work. Homer could not leave the reader under a painful impression.

The subject of the "Odyssey" being the return of Ulysses, the poem should be over when Ulysses arrives at Ithaca; but, can we consider it as a fault that the poet has shown, before finishing, the restoration of the hero to his throne and the punishment of the suitors?

3. In regard to the consistency of the characters: some of them are found in both poems, and they are strikingly consistent with each other. The characters of Achilles, Agamemnon, Menelaus, Nestor, Ajax, Diomede, Ulysses, Hector, Priam, Paris, Helen, Hecuba, and Andromache in the "Iliad," those of Telemachus, Penelope, Euryclea, Nausicaa, and Eumæus, in the "Odyssey," are perfectly drawn and consistent throughout. Then, Homer is the writer of both poems. If not, we must admit that in a short space of time two

men existed who, contrary to any thing that has ever been seen in the world, wrote an epic poem; or, we must admit another thing more improbable, that the lays of many bards, living at different epochs, being united, have produced the most wonderful literary work.

In conclusion, we might admit that Homer used for the compositions of his works many legends, composed in Asia Minor, about the gods and their interference in the Trojan war, and composed the "Iliad" and the "Odyssey," and that these poems, learned by heart and repeated by singers, were at length collected, and, with few interpolations, set in order under Pisistratus.

A few words from St. Augustine may properly be placed here: "Homer," said he, "will have no temples, nor games, nor sacrifices in Christendom; but his statue is yet to be seen in the palaces of kings, and his name will remain in honor among the nations to the world's end. He stands, by prescription, alone and aloft on Parnassus, where it is not possible now that any human genius should stand with him, the father and the prince of all heroic poets, the boast and the glory of his own Greece, and the love and admiration of all mankind."

Whatever may be the opinion which we form about the reality of the Trojan war, we must admit that Homer cannot be accepted as an historian; but, the picture which he gives of the manners and creed of his epoch is extremely precious. Homer did not compose the fifty hymns attributed to him, neither the Batrachomyomachy nor the Margites.

CHAPTER IV.

DIDACTIC POETRY.

Hesiod.—He was born at Ascra, in Bœotia; by descent he was an Asiatic Greek. The same sadness and gloom which distinguish the climate of Ascra from that of the coast of Asia, mark the poetry of Hesiod. The romantic ideal of the Homeric age gives place to the stern reality of common life and daily duty. His description of the lot of humanity is less brilliant, but more true. Impressed with a sense of the social evils of his time, Hesiod looks for a remedy; his purpose is didactic and moral. Hesiod lived some time after Homer, about 900 years B. C. He borrowed much from the great epic poet.

His works are—1. Ἔργα καὶ Ἡμέραι ("Works and Days"). Its leading subject is the various occupations and duties of life, in its several relations, with a conclusion consisting of a calendar for the use of agriculturists and navigators. 2. A "Theogony, or a History of the Origin of the World and the Genealogies of the Gods;" a work important and interesting in a mythological point of view. 3. "The Eœæ" (Μεγαλαί Ἡοῖαι), "ἢ οἴη, such as were," a formula with which many of the descriptions were introduced. This work contained the history of the favorites of the gods. 4. Κατάλογος Γυναικῶν ("The Catalogue of Women"), a book distinct from "The Eœæ," and containing the genealogies of celebrated women of the heroic age. 5. Ἀσπίς Ἡρακλέους ("The Shield of Hercules"). This last work is probably a composition belonging to another poet. These last three poems formed one work, attributed to Hesiod, and called "The Heroogony." The last part, or "The Shield of Hercules," is a fragment attached to it by some unknown rhapsodist. It is the only part remaining of "The Heroogony;" few fragments of the other parts have been preserved.

Hesiod is admired for the elegance of his diction, and the sweetness of his poetry. It may be said of him, what he was saying of a poet, γλυκερὴ ῥέει αὐδή (his voice flows sweet). Like Homer he wrote in the Ionic dialect, with some Æolisms intermingled.

Homer and Hesiod are the principal poets of the epic cycle; for, although we have spoken of Hesiod as a didactic poet, a great part of his writings possess the epic character. We will give here the names of several writers who belong to the same era, but whose works are lost. They are:

Arctinus of Miletus.—He has been called a disciple of Homer. His poem consisted of 9,100 verses. He related the events of the Trojan war, following the death of Hector.

Lesches of Lesbos.—He lived, like Arctinus, at the time of Archilochus, in the eighteenth Olympiad, 708. He composed the "Little Iliad" (Ἰλίας Μικρά)

Agias of Trœzen.—He lived in 740, and the ancients, referring to his poem, say: Ὁ τοὺς νόστους γραψάς; hence we conclude that the title of his work was "Νόστοι," which work contained the history of the return of the Achæans from Troy.

Eumelus of Corinth.—He lived in the third Olympiad, and wrote a history of Corinth in heroic verse.

Strasinus of Cyprus.—We have a few verses of a poem from that writer, which was entitled Τὰ Κυπρία ἔπη (" The Cyprian Epics ").

The number of poems in the epic style written at that time amounts to thirty, relating mostly to the Trojan war, the history of Thebes, and the exploits of Hercules.

CHAPTER V.

ELEGIAC AND IAMBIC POETRY.

AUTHORS do not agree about the etymology of the words "elegy" and "iamb." The first deviation from the heroic hexameter took place two hundred years after Homer. Callinus of Ephesus was the first who gave the elegiac stanza. It was used for monumental and other inscriptions, "ἐπιγραμμάτα," wherever brevity of expression required terseness and conciseness. This metre, used only for treating subjects breathing a melancholy, and also a warlike and patriotic, spirit, soon degenerated, and Archilochus gave, in that same metre, the earliest specimens of what is called in modern times "the Anacreontic," celebrating the delights of wine and revelry.

The poets who wrote in the elegiac form, and whose works are almost entirely lost, were :

Callinus of Ephesus.—He lived about 720 B. C.

Tyrtæus.—He was born at Athens in 685. We have from this poet, who had been sent, through derision by the Athenians, as a commander to the Spartans, several fragments remaining of his elegies. They are written in the Ionic dialect, and are full of enthusiastic and patriotic feelings. His anapæstic marches were written in Doric; of these only one single fragment came down to us. For all the fragments from Tyrtæus you may see the "Anthologia."

Archilochus of Paros.—He lived in 688. He was regarded by the ancients as one of the greatest poets that Greece ever produced. Cicero classes him with Homer, Sophocles, and Pindar. His best composition was a hymn in honor of Hercules. He must be blamed, however, for the bitterness and vindictive spirit which characterize his verses, and the indecency which pervades them. Many fragments of his compositions may be found in the "Anthologia."

Simonides of Amorgos.—There have been two poets of the name of Simonides. The one mentioned here lived in 664, and was called the Ἰαμβογράφος. We have only one fragment from his writings. It is a satiric piece, simple and elegant, entitled "Περὶ Γυναικῶν."

Mimnermus of Smyrna.—He lived at the time of Solon, 594.

The Athenian **Theognis** was born in 583. We have many fragments of his elegies, in all 1,392 verses, which were popular songs exercising a great influence at the time. Theognis was the poet of the old aristocracy, which was crumbling away before the growing power of the wealthier commons, led by some influential citizen, called in Greece "tyrant." Theognis lived at the time of the thirty tyrants.

The last two were **Xenophanes of Ælea,** the founder

of the Æleatic school of philosophy (540), and **Phocylides of Miletus,** whose compositions are all introduced by the words, " And this, too, is Phocylides."

Καὶ τόδε Φωκυλίδεω. Λέριοι κακοί, οὐκ ὁ μέν, ὅς δ' οὐ,
Πάντες πλὴν Προκλέους, καὶ Προκλέης Λέριος.

The iambic verse was invented by Archilochus of Paros. One characteristic of iambic verse is rapidity; it is well suited for repartee and satire.

"Archilocum proprio rabies armavit iambo,"

says Horace; and again—

" In celeres iambos misit furentem."

The iambic verse became one of the elements of the Attic drama. Archilochus was not only an iambic poet—we have seen that he wrote elegies. He is also the inventor of the Ἐπώδος, so well imitated by Horace. We may see that Greek poetry is progressing in the development of its form, and reaching maturity in lyric poetry. The first writers in iambic poetry were, besides Archilochus and Simonides, of whom we have spoken :

Hipponax of Ephesus, the inventor of the choliambic or lame iambic, because the last foot was a spondee; and **Æsop,** born in 620, according to some authors, whose fables exist and are much known: he was probably a slave, and lived at the time of Crœsus, and at the court of that prince. Anthon pretends that Æsop did not write fables; compositions of that nature were written by many poets, who handed them down by tradition, and they were collected afterward, as it has been done by Demetrius Phalereus, in 150, and by Babrius, in 150 B. C. It is useless to relate here the narrative of Plutarch concerning the death of Æsop, since we may seriously doubt whether Æsop has ever existed.*

CHAPTER VI.

LYRIC POETRY.

LYRIC poetry is the outpouring of the human heart, when inspired either by religion or love. The former characterizes the lyric of the Dorians, the latter that of the Æolians. The choral lyric of the Dorians was eminently fitted for solemn and sacred subjects; for accompanying the dignified march of the priests, and the cheerful dance of the assistant band of youths and

* Music was imperfectly known in Greece. The word ἁρμονική (harmony) did not mean at that time what it meant since; it was simply the art of melody, that is, the singing with two voices separated by one octave, the natural distance between the pitch of a female voice and of a male voice. Until 648 they had only the lyre tetrachord, making the distances one-fourth. Terpander, a native of Lesbos, was the inventor of the real science of harmony, and introduced in the lyre three more chords. This new compass was called Διὰ πασῶν through all the sounds. He is the first who adapted melodies to the national lays of the Lacedæmonians.

Μέλος πρῶτος περιέθηκε τοῖς ποιήμασι,
Καὶ τοὺς Λακεδαιμονίων νόμους ἐμελοποίησε.

Terpander may be considered as the founder of Greek musical science, and he flourished just at the time when lyric poetry was developing itself.

virgins, while the Æolian measures and dialect were more suitable to express human sentiment and passion. The deities, in whose honor choral odes, accompanied with music and dancing, were sung, were Apollo and Bacchus. The earliest choral song was the "Pæan," a song of joy, as it is evinced by the exclamation "ἰή," which precedes it.

The other choral songs were: (νόμοι) the nomes, lyric hymns in honor of Apollo; (ὑπορχημάτα) the hyporchemes, songs accompanying the pantomimic dances, which bore the same name; (παρθένια) the parthenia, modest songs sung by young virgins; (προσοδία) hymns sung as the procession of priests marched toward the altar; (διθύραμβος) the dithyramb was a poem in honor of Dionysus. It has been the germ of the choral element in Attic tragedy. The authors do not agree about the etymology, but probably it comes from Διός and θύρσος. The thyrsus was emblematic of Dionysus wrapped in ivy.

The distinction between the two schools cannot be maintained when treating of convivial poetry, for poems of this kind were written both by Æolians and Dorians. Those compositions were called σκολία; these songs, which enlivened the banquet, were sometimes joyous and voluptuous, and not unfrequently coarse and licentious.

We may give, as an example of this species of composition, the two following stanzas from two scholia of Simonides the Younger:

> Συνετῶν ἐστὶν ἀνδρῶν
> Πρὶν γενέσθαι τὰ δυσχερῆ

Προνοῆσαι ὅπως μὴ γένηται·
'Ανδρείων δέ, γενόμενα εὖ θέσθαι.

'Υγιαίνειν μὲν ἄριστον ἀνδρὶ θνατῷ·
Δεύτερον δέ, καλὸν φυὰν γενέσθαι
Τὸ τρίτον δέ, πλουτεῖν ἀδόλως·
Καὶ τὸ τέταρτον, ἡβᾶν μετὰ τῶν φίλων.

To these compositions we must add (ἐπιθαλάμια) the epithalamia, songs which were sung at marriages in honor of the bride.

The following are the names of the lyric poets of that period. Nine of them were placed by the Alexandrian grammarians in their canon, and they are designated here by the numbers placed before their names:

Eumelus, born at Corinth, in 768; he was certainly the author of a lyric composition, a prosodion, in honor of Apollo.

1. **Alcman,** born in 671, at Sardis; he was brought as a slave to Sparta. He wrote many parthenia; in all, he composed six books of poems, but the few fragments which remain scarcely allow us to judge how far he deserves the great reputation which he acquired. Some of his verses, however, display a true poetical spirit. (*See* the "Anthology.")

Arion was a native of Lesbos; he lived in 628, and is very likely the inventor of the dithyramb. He drowned himself, his life being threatened by the sailors, while he was returning to Corinth.

2. **Alcæus** was born at Mytilene, in 610. The struggle between aristocracy and democracy, which was the curse of Greece at that time, obliged him to leave his

country. The few fragments of Alcæus's compositions
show a lofty character, a great conciseness of style, and
clearness of images. Alcæus was the inventor of the
metre that bears his name, one of the most beautiful
and melodious of all the lyric measures. Horace imitated Alcæus in his best compositions. He wrote:
1. Hymns, relating legends of the gods; 2. Songs of
love and wine; 3. Party-songs. Horace took from
him the subjects of his fourteenth and thirty-seventh
odes, first book.

3. **Sappho,** a woman of Lesbos, living in 610, of the
liveliest fancy and most ardent passions. She was
much calumniated, and, very likely, through jealousy.
She wrote hymns and epithalamia. She has been imitated by Horace, in his lighter and softer poems. Her
life, like that of many other Lesbian women of talent
and refinement, was passed in literary pursuits; in the
midst of a circle of female friends and pupils of her
own sex. Besides elegies and iambics, she wrote nine
books of lyric poems, and invented the plectrum. All
that has reached us of her compositions consist of: 1.
A beautiful ode to Venus, in the Sapphic measure;
2. A second ode in the same measure, and still more
beautiful, a description of the tumultuous emotions of
love; 3. Various fragments, all unfortunately very
short, found in Aristotle, Plutarch, Athenæus, and
others; 4. Three epigrams.

The authors do not agree about her death, but she
killed herself by a leap from the Leucadian promontory.
The following is the epigram extant in her honor:

'Εννέα τὰς Μούσας φασίν τινες· ὡς ὀλιγώρως·
'Ηνῖδε καὶ Σαπφὼ Λεσβόθεν ἡ δικάτη.

Erinna, born at Rhodes, in 610; she was a friend of Sappho, and a very distinguished poetess, but she wrote rather in the epic style. She has been surnamed the " Bee," on account of the sweetness of her verse. Only four lines remain of her " Distaff."

4. **Stesichorus.**—He was born at Himera (Sicily), in 632, and died in 560. Some traditions make him a son of Hesiod, and it is easy to explain that apparent anachronism, for, like the Homerides, we have the Hesiodides—they were the admirers of Hesiod, who affected the title of sons of that poet. Stesichorus was the first who adapted epic subjects to lyric verses; he was the first also who invested the bucolic, or pastoral, with a classical character. He has been imitated by Theocritus, and in later times by Virgil, who gave to these compositions a didactic form. Stesichorus belonged to a Dorian family established in Sicily, and, as we may see, the bucolic has a Dorian origin as far as its classical character is concerned, for it is impossible to discover who used it for the first time.

5. **Ibycus,** a native of Rhegium, born in 540. A tradition relates that he was slain by robbers, and his death avenged by cranes; nothing is left of his poems.

6. **Anacreon** was born at Teos, in 540, and, soon after his birth, his family migrated to Abdera. He was a sensualist, and his poems, like those of a band of poets who lived at the court of Hipparchus, were all voluptuous and sensualistic. He died at the age of eighty-five years, very likely by accident.

7. **Simonides,** born at Ceos, in 556. He was the grandson of the elegiac poet of the same name. He spent many years at the court of Hipparchus, and was

a good lyric poet, but inferior to Pindar. He is unri-valled for the neatness and elegance of his epigrams; he composed many epitaphs, some of which have been preserved, and one of them is well known to every reader of Thucydides. Several elegies of Simonides may be seen in the "Anthology;" they were used as plaintive songs for the death of individuals. In those pieces the poet laments, with heart-felt pathos, the death of persons dear to him; among these are the beautiful verses concerning Gorgo, who, while dying, utters these words to her mother: "Remain here with my father, and become, with a happier fate, the mother of another daughter, who may tend thee in thy old age." What may be added to the credit of Simonides is, that he was victorious at Athens, over Æschylus, in an elegy in honor of those who fell at Marathon. Simonides was surely a great master of the pathetic.

8. **Bacchylides.**—He was born also at Ceos, and lived at the court of Hiero, with Simonides and Pindar. His lyrics were much appreciated for their ethical value, and exhibited polish, correctness, and delicacy, but not the fire of fervor of Pindar. Let us take, among several fragments preserved in the "Anthology," the fol-lowing:

> Λυδία μὲν γὰρ λίθος
> Μανύει χρυσόν·
> Ἀνδρῶν δ' ἀρετὴν
> Σοφίαν τε παγκρατὴς
> Ἐλέγχει ἀλήθεια.

Corinna was born at Thebes, and was living at the time of Pindar. She was distinguished for her skill in lyric verses, and remarkable for her personal attractions. While Pindar was still a young man she was his rival, and gained the victory over him no less than five times. She has been surnamed "the Fly" (*Μυΐα*). Too few fragments are extant of her writings, in order to form a correct judgment of her abilities as a lyric poetess.

9. **Pindar.**—The independent existence of Dorian lyric poetry ceased with this poet. The drama commenced with Æschylus. Although Pindar belongs to

PINDAR.

the first period, the time in which he lived was well fitted for the development of his genius. Athens and Greece had reached the climax of power, and, of course, of pride.

Pindar was born at Cynocephalæ, a village near Thebes, in 517. He went early to Athens. His tenth "Pythian," written in 502, when he was only fifteen years old, spread widely his reputation. After having

spent four years at the court of Hiero, that great friend
of poets, he came back to Greece and lived at Thebes,
where he died, at the age of eighty. Pindar is undoubtedly the greatest lyric poet of Greece. He wrote
every kind of lyric songs; his way of treating a subject was very peculiar; no one could develop his ideas
more beautifully, and his odes contain many moral con-
siderations. They are the only compositions extant;
they are admired for sublimity of sentiments, grandeur
of expression, energy and magnificence of style, boldness of metaphors, harmony of numbers, and elegance
of diction. We have, remaining at the present day,
forty-five of the "Epinicia," or triumphal odes, together with some few fragments of his other productions. The "Epinicia" are divided into four classes,
or kinds, and derive their names respectively from the
four great games of Greece. Thus we have: 1. "Olympic Odes," to the number of fourteen; 2. "Pythian
Odes," to the number of twelve; 3. "Nemean Odes,"
eleven in number; and, 4. "Isthmian Odes," amount-
ing to eight. The following criticism of Pindar is
found in Horace:

> "Monte decurrens velut amnis, imbres
> Quem super notas aluere ripas,
> Fervet, immensusque ruit profundo
> Pindarus ore."   —*Ode* iv., 2.

In the opening of this ode, Horace says that Pindar's powers defy imitation or rivalry:

> "Pindarum quisquis studet æmulari,
> Iule, ceratis ope Dædalea
> Nititur pennis, vitreo daturus
> Nomina ponto."   —*Ode* iv., 2.

CHAPTER VII.

PROSE WRITERS : LAWS—HISTORY.

POETRY constituted the only literature in the period of mingled rudeness and refinement which lies between barbarism and advanced civilization. It is the natural language of the heart and imagination, and it recognizes no artificial limitations. Prose writing, on the contrary, requires a greater ripeness of intellect and language. Some subjects cannot be treated conveniently in poetry. Prose was gradually introduced as soon as society required more writing for its formation. The essays in prose writing, which were written before Pisistratus, were legislative, historical, and philosophical. At the end of the seventh century, revolutions were taking place in the main cities of Greece; monarchies were decaying, and aristocracy struggling against democracy. Serious men turned their attention to the means of remedying those evils, hence the legislators. Still we find that the first laws are written in verses. It was the time of the seven wise men— Thales, Bias, Pittacus, Solon, Cleobulus, Chilo, and Periander—from 665–540.

The names of those who wrote ordinances and laws, and who belonged to the school of Solon, of whom some worked with him, are :

Periander (627), who was tyrant of Corinth for forty-four years; his ordinances display large views, but, according to Herodotus, he was very cruel.

Pittacus (652), a native of Mytilene. Besides a prose

work in defence of his laws, he wrote six hundred elegiac verses; he was for ten years tyrant of Lesbos, and
died in 569. Some of his maxims and precepts are
beautiful.

Thales was born at Miletus, in 635; he became the
founder of the Ionian philosophy. Aristotle considers
him as the first discoverer of mathematics and physical
philosophy. Thales studied that science in Egypt,
under the priests of Memphis. Quotations from his
writings are found frequently in Aristotle.

Solon (638).—He was born at Salamis. He became
archon and legislator in 594. Solon was distinguished
not only as a legislator, but also as a philosopher ; he
owes much to his travels. By his exertions he per-
suaded the Athenians to take back Salamis, which had
been snatched from them by the Megarians. That circumstance made him acquire much influence at Athens,
and Solon, finding that much disorder existed there,
gave to the Athenians a new constitution, which reme-
died the evils suffered, especially by those who were in
debt. His system was overthrown at the time of the
usurpation of Pisistratus. Nothing is left of his writings in prose. In regard to his poetry, we have some
fragments, and the finest is his " Prayer to the Muses."

Three more names should be added, in order to
complete our list : Cleobulus (638), who was tyrant of
Rhodes; Bias (550), the tyrant of Priene (Ionia); and
Chilos (596), the ephor of Sparta. We have no writings from them.*

* It seems but natural that we should say a few words about
the great legislator of Sparta, Lycurgus. Although he did not
write his laws, still his name must be mentioned, because very

In the historical division we have only three names of writers, whose works are not extant. Before them, as we have said, poets were the only historians; their songs celebrated in verse historical facts, but mingled with fables, and consequently of no reliance. Still, their writings constitute the only materials we have for the history of the period before the seventh century. The three writers of history before Pisistratus were:

Cadmus, 540.—This Cadmus was a native of Miletus, and ought not to be confounded with Cadmus, the son of Agenor, who introduced the alphabet into Greece. He wrote a work on the colonization of Ionia, and the foundation of Miletus. The book is lost. According to Socrates, he is the first who bore the title of σόφιστης.

Acusilaus.—This historian was born at Argos, and lived a short time previous to the Persian invasion of Greece. He wrote legends of mythologies and genealogies. His writings, except a few fragments, are also lost.

Hecateus, born at Miletus, in 540. The references

likely all the legislators who came after him have found in Lycurgus's ordinances much useful information. Lycurgus lived in the ninth century before the Christian era. According to Plutarch, he left Sparta in order to avoid suspicion, and visited Crete and Egypt, studied the laws and customs of those countries, and, returning to Sparta, he reformed the legislation of his native place. In order to prevent his countrymen from destroying the result of his labors and efforts, he left Sparta, having made the citizens swear that they would not change any thing in the constitution which he had published, and which they had accepted, before his return. Lycurgus never did come back, and Sparta was flourishing as long as it remained faithful to his laws.

to his work show that he was a voluminous writer; we have only a few fragments from him. He wrote genealogies, and gave much information about geography; but little credit can be given to those sources.

CHAPTER VIII.

PROSE—PHILOSOPHY.

PHILOSOPHY owed its origin among the Greeks to the Greek mind, and not to foreign influence.

Pherecydes of Syros (600) was the first philosopher. His system, like all the systems of that time, is confused. We have only extracts, and we might say that no system is given, but only unconnected thoughts. Pherecydes says that $Ζεὺς$, $Χρόνος$, and $Γῆ$, exist from all eternity. It was a good beginning, evidently taken from some biblical reminiscence. But he does not draw any reasonable conclusions. Aristotle says of Pherecydes, that he stands on the boundary-line between mythical poetry and philosophy. "Zeus," he writes, "Chronos, and Chthonia, existed from eternity. Chthonia was called Ge. Zeus then transforms himself into Eros, the god of Love, wishing to form the world from the original materials made by Chronos and Ge. Zeus makes a large and beautiful garment; upon it he paints Earth and Ogenos (Ocean), and the horses of Ogenos, and he spreads the garment over a winged oak." This is evidently poetry, although expressed in prose. As we see, there is in him assertion, and no speculation. His assertion was the germ from which philosophy was developed, but not philosophy. Very little is known about his life, and we know nothing certain in regard to the way that he died. The first who gave a system of philosophy was Thales. The notion that Greek philosophy is derived from Oriental philosophy has been widely spread and defended, but it cannot be admitted. For, if such were the case, there would be want of unity; there is no trace of any want of connection, which would necessarily result from the introduction of a foreign element. Besides this first consideration, Eastern philosophy would have taught Greece more perfect notions respecting the personality of the Deity; would have accustomed the Greek mind to contemplate the divine power as creative; would have defined more clearly the dealings of men with God. These subjects did not form a part of Greek philosophy. Deity was little more than an abstract principle of reason. Matter was as eternal as God. God did not interfere in the concerns or interests of man. As we may see, there is much difference between the philosophies of those two races.

In investigating the history of Greek philosophical literature, a striking point of resemblance is observable between it and their poetical literature—a resemblance arising out of the national character itself. The Greek philosophy followed this division of the Greek poetry. We have the Ionian school, the most vivid one, but limiting itself to the study of physical phenomena, the school where imagination is more glowing; and the Dorian school, which is more serious, and examines especially the principles of moral philosophy. This school, founded in Magna Græcia, gave birth to the Aleatic school, established at Alea (Magna Græcia), by Xenophanes.

The philosophy of that time may be divided into two parts, dynamical and mechanical. The first attributes to the atoms a power of moving and acting, *Δύναμις;* the other refuses that power to the elements of things, and attributes the changes to some external force. To the first school belong Thales, Anaximenes, Diogenes, and Heraclitus; in the second, we find Anaximander, Anaxagoras, and Archelaus, the teacher of Socrates. The following are the philosophers from whom we have fragments, or quotations, or references, and who belong more properly to the history of ancient literature:

Already we have spoken of **Thales.** That philosopher gave water as the principle of every thing; but, by water, he understood very likely the chaos, or the material substances in dissolution.

Anaximander, born in 610, at Miletus, as we have said, was a mechanical philosopher. According to him, the principle (*ἀρχή*) of every thing is the infinite (*τὸ ἄπειρον*); a mixture (*μίγμα*) of elements out of which substances are formed by separation, the homogeneous parts being attracted toward each other. The cause of the production of animated beings is the solar heat.

Anaximenes was also a native of Miletus, where he was born in 556. He pretended that from air all things were produced. We have no fragments of the writings of those two philosophers, but many references to their systems may be found in the writings of Aristotle.

Diogenes was a pupil of Anaximenes, and a native of Apollonia, in Crete. He took the views of his master, in regard to the primal element of every thing. He wrote several books on cosmology (περὶ φύσεως). The fragments which remain have been recently collected and edited.

Anaxagoras was also a pupil of Anaximenes. He died at Lampsacus, after a very stormy life. Few fragments remain of his writings, which have been more numerous than those of Diogenes; from those fragments we may see that Anaxagoras had a good knowledge of astronomy.

Heraclitus was born at Ephesus, in the sixty-ninth Olympiad. He was very obscure in his style, and has been surnamed on that account σκοτεινός. Heraclitus was a misanthrope by nature; his philosophy has especially a moral character; still, it treats of the formation of the world, and belongs to the dynamical school. God is found everywhere. Fire is the original element of the material world. We have many fragments of his work, Περὶ φύσεως. Heraclitus is the first who taught the pantheistic doctrine. His style is, besides being obscure, too concise and broken.

Archelaus was a pupil of Anaxagoras, whose principles he accepted, and became the teacher of Socrates. He has been called Φυσικός (the Natural Philosopher). We have little information about his life, and no fragment is extant of his writings.

Pythagoras was probably a native of Samos, where he was born in the forty-ninth Olympiad. He travelled much, and fixed himself at Crotona, in Magna Græcia. He was the first who took the name of Philosopher. In politics he was aristocratic, and, by his influence, the aristocratic government was established at Crotona and its vicinity. It was in that place that Pythagoras founded his famous school, which had as many as six hundred pupils, living together, and preparing themselves to reach the degree of Esoterics. The government established at Crotona by the influence of Pythagoras was upset, and the philosopher had to fly; he reached Metapontum, but there he was killed. Many books have been attributed to him by modern Pythagoreans; they are evidently spurious, and the mixture of the ancient and modern Pythagorean doctrine makes it difficult to determine what the real teaching of Pythagoras was. It is not probable that Pythagoras attributed to number the meaning given to it afterward, going so far as to make number the principle of matter. But it is clear that Pythagoras considered number as the principle of physical as well as moral harmony in the world—and he establishes his system for any kind of sciences or beings—and so number is the essence (οὐσια) and principle (ἀρχή) of all things. But, once more, essence is not the substance (ΰλη) in the sense of Pythagoras. Pythagoras admits the unity of God, and the immortality of the soul; he taught, but did not invent, the doctrine of metempsychosis. We have no writing from Pythagoras; the details concerning his life, his institutes, and his doctrine, have been preserved by his disciples.

Xenophanes.—This elegiac poet, who founded the Eleatic school, was born at Colophon, in 556. Xenophanes has exact notions about God and his attributes. He most probably was not a pantheist. Xenophanes asserts that God is the same as the universe, but he also asserts the existence of a material world distinct from God. Did he mean that God was a spiritual substance pervading the material universe? It is impossible to determine. The Eleatic school showed a great improvement: 1. In asserting the unity of God; 2. In referring the conclusions of the other systems to the test of reason. We have no writings from Xenophanes

BOOK II.

CHAPTER I.

DRAMATIC STYLE—ITS INFANCY.

THE period at which Greece began to have a fixed
and established national literature was that of Pisistratus (529, the time of his death), commonly called
the Tyrant of Athens. The administration of the
tyrants was the transition from the aristocratic and
oligarchic to the democratic government. This was
a flourishing time for Greece. Pisistratus's power
lasted ten years, and, during that time, the drama made
its appearance; it was rude in its infancy, but prom-
ising its future greatness. The union of epic and lyric
style formed dramatic poetry.

The drama is the creation of the Hellenic race; we
do not find it among the Semitic families, and the Romans have imitated the Greeks.

There are two characteristic features in the Attic
drama: First, it is essentially religious. The drama
was a ceremonial for the public worship of some di-

vinity. This character of the drama has been kept always. The believers in a pure faith can scarcely understand a religious element in dramatic exhibitions. They who know that God is a spirit feel that his attributes are too awful to permit any ideas connected with the Deity to be brought into contact with the exhibition of human passions. But the imaginative Greek did not experience this difficulty. His gods were either the creatures of his own fancy, or they were human beings like himself, who had, while alive, attained the heroic standard, and after death had been deified. They possessed the same properties, feelings, passions, and moral imperfections, as himself; even the supreme ruler of them all was not omnipotent. His own native land was theirs—they were his fellow-countrymen, as it were. He could bathe in the river, or drink of the fountain, or seek shade in the grove, or climb the hills, which were pervaded by the influence and consecrated by the presence of deity. Parnassus, where the Muses, the authors of all inspiration, resided, was close at hand. The mighty Olympus, the dwelling-place of Zeus himself, he might behold with his own eyes. The second character of the drama was the realization of the audience, represented by the chorus, which personified the audience. The chorus was of course supposed to enter into the feelings and fortunes, and express the sympathies, of the audience.

We find two parts in the drama, the chorus and the dialogue. The first one, which was almost entirely lyric, was Dorian, and the other one was Ionian. This peculiarity has been explained before. Although the chorus was an important element of the drama, still

3

the dialogue constituted its essence. How was the dialogue connected with the original chorus? In order to solve that question, let us see the origin of the drama. Aristotle says that tragedy was first a speech delivered between the dances, by the ballet-master dressed in a goat-skin (τράγος). These speeches, or narratives, were first connected with some event in the life of Bacchus. By degrees the subject of these speeches was changed, and this modification was introduced by Thespis, the real inventor of tragedy, 550. By degrees also the mysteries of Eleusis were introduced, in order to correct the indecencies of Bacchus's festivities. Thespis introduced a performer who was not the ballet-master. Phrynicus, and after him Chærilus, followed him in his modifications (523–511); the legends of Bacchus were abandoned, and Phrynicus introduced the satyric element in the drama. Pratinas is the one who introduced pure satyric dramas. These three men were the forerunners of the great dramatists, and even Chærilus and Pratinas contended with Æschylus in 499. It was then the time of the great tragic writers, but most of the works of the dramatists have been lost. We have but few tragedies from Æschylus, Sophocles, and Euripides. Chærilus, who was born in 523, may be considered as having probably developed the satyric drama, introduced by his contemporary Phrynicus, if we may place any confidence in the following verse of an anonymous poet:

'Ηνίκα μὲν βασιλεὺς ἦν Χοιρίλος ἐν Σατύροις.

During forty years Chærilus continued his exhibition of tragedies, and during that time he produced one hundred and fifty pieces, and gained thirteen victories. Although Chærilus developed the satyric drama, it was not he, but Pratinas, who completed the separation between the tragic and satyric drama.

CHAPTER II.

DRAMATIC STYLE—ITS PERFECTION.

THE time of Pericles (500–425) exhibits the dramatic style in its perfection. Although the three great dramatists of Greece were imbued with the spirit of Homer, still they were as creative as Homer himself; they were the representatives of the religious belief of their time, and they had of the deity a more divine notion than the great epic poet. Like Homer and Pindar, they represent a poetic era.

Æschylus.—He was born in 525, at Eleusis, in Attica, and was the son of Euphorion. He devoted himself to poetry at an early age, but did not succeed much until 484. He was vanquished by Sophocles. Æschylus was a soldier for several years, and fought at Marathon and Salamis, and, in these two engagements, he distinguished himself for his bravery. The following epigram shows it :

’Αλκήν δ’ εὐδόκιμον Μαραθώνιον ἄλσος ἂν εἴπου·
Καὶ βαθυχαιτήεις Μῆδος ἐπιστάμενος.

The Athenians exiled him, under the pretence of impiety. He died by accident; an eagle dropped a tortoise on his head, which was bald, mistaking it for a rock. We find the following epitaph on his tomb:

Αἰσχύλον Εὐφορίονος ᾿Αθηναῖον τόδε κεύθει
Μνῆμα καταφθύμενον πορυφόροιο Γέλας
᾿Αλκήν δ᾿ εὐδόκιμον, κ. τ. λ.

Æschylus wrote seventy tragedies, of which only seven are extant. They were trilogies; that is, each subject comprised three tragedies. Æschylus has been called the "Father of Tragedy," on account of the many improvements which he introduced on the stage. In philosophical sentiments Æschylus is said to have been a Pythagorean, and in his extant dramas the tenets of this sect may be occasionally traced, as, deep veneration in what concerns the gods, high regard for the sanctity of an oath and the nuptial bond, and the immortality of the soul. Aristophanes, depicting Æschylus, says that his temper was stern, proud, and impatient; his sentiments, pure, noble, and warlike; his genius, inventive, magnificent, and towering, even to occasional extravagance; his style, bold, lofty, and impetuous, full of gorgeous imagery and ponderous expression, while, in the dramatic arrangement of his pieces, there remained much of ancient simplicity, and somewhat even of uncouth rudeness. He is similar to Dante and Shakespeare, in the peculiar strangeness of his imaginations and expressions. Æschylus ranked supreme in tragedy.

With the portrait thus drawn by Aristophanes, the opinions of the ancient critics in general coincide. He has been praised especially by Dionysius of Halicarnassus, Longinus, and by Quintilian. We must add, however, that the tragic style of Æschylus is far from perfect, and frequently deviates into the epic and the lyric. It is often abrupt, disproportioned, and harsh. The tragedies extant of Æschylus are:

1. "The Persians." It was the second of a trilogy, in which the poet was celebrating the triumph of Greece over Persia.

2. "The Seven against Thebes." This tragedy also was the second of a trilogy, where Æschylus exhibits the results of the curse of Œdipus pronounced against his sons, Eteocles and Polynices. In these two tragedies the poet pours forth a warlike strain; the personal inclination of Æschylus for the life of a hero beams forth in a manner which cannot be mistaken.

3. "The Suppliants." It was the second of a trilogy, and embodied the history of the house of Danaus. This play forms one of the feeblest productions of Æschylus; the chorus in it plays the principal character.

4. "Prometheus Bound." This piece exhibits a terrible example of the wrath and revenge of Zeus; all the personages were divinities. It was also the second of a trilogy, of which the first was "Prometheus the Fire-Bringer," and the third "Prometheus Unbound."

5. We have here a complete trilogy—"Agamemnon," "Chœphori," and "Eumenides." These tragedies embodied the legend of Orestes revenging the death of his father by killing his mother Clytemnestra. The choruses in "Agamemnon" are beautiful, particularly when Æschylus shows the struggle between the duties of a chief and the affections of a father, in reference to the sacrifice of Iphigenia. Orestes is in these

tragedies an application of the law of blood-guilt; upon him was devolving the duty of executing vengeance upon the murderer of his father. After the parricidal deed committed by Orestes, no human power can take vengeance upon him, because he is the avenger of blood; his mother's furies can alone pursue him, and even they are powerless when he has visited the shrine of Delphi as a suppliant for purification. As soon as he has received it at the hands of the god, the furies become well-disposed " Eumenides."

Sophocles.—He was born at Colonos, near Athens, in 495. No one surpassed Æschylus for boldness and genius; no one surpassed Sophocles for perfection of language and composition. This quality procured for him the title of "The Attic Bee." The characters of Æschylus have generally an awful and superhuman vastness; Sophocles depicts real life; Æschylus excites terror and admiration, Sophocles excites sympathy and affection. He wrote verses at a very early age, and was held in great esteem by his countrymen. He received a high military command, but soon showed that he was better qualified for writing verses than leading an army. It is not known how he died. Some verses are found in the "Anthologia," which are contradictory. We read first:

> Ἐσβέσθης, γηραιὲ Σοφόκλεες, ἄνθος ἀοιδῶν,
> Οἰνωπὸν Βάκχου βότρυν ἐρεπτόμενος.

This epigram is from Simonides. It is said elsewhere that Sophocles died in the exercise of his beloved art, in extreme old age, without disease and without suffering:

> Καλῶς ετελεύτησ' οὐδὲν ὑπομείνας κακόν.

The first epigram is probably the true one. We may rely for this on the saying of Aristophanes, although he sometimes exaggerates. The comic poet shows us Sophocles fond of wine and pleasure; he says in his "Ranæ," speaking of him:

'Ο δ' εὔκολος μὲν ἐνθάδε, εὔκολος δ' ἐκεῖ.

In the tragedies of Sophocles is seen the perfection of the Greek drama, and this does not contradict what has been asserted above. Although Aristotle pronounces Euripides to be the most tragic of poets, and Longinus pronounces him to have been unequalled in his tragic representations of love and madness, yet no tragic poet equalled Sophocles in combining dignity, purity, pathos, and piety, with the most refined genius and the highest poetical talent. Seven tragedies only are extant out of one hundred and thirteen, and we have probably the best ones. They are, in order of merit:

1. "Œdipus Rex" (Οἰδίπους τύραννος). It would be difficult to conceive a subject more thoroughly tragical than that which forms the basis of this play. The "Œdipus Tyrannus" is considered not only as the *chef-d'œuvre* of Sophocles, but also as the finest tragedy of antiquity.

2. "Antigone" ('Αντίγονη). The sister of Poly- nices, she disobeys Cleon and buries her brother. Her answers to Cleon are sometimes sublime, when Cleon accuses Polynices of hatred toward him. "Oh, no!" exclaims Antigone, "he was born to love, not to hate."

Οὐ τοι συνεχθείν, αλλὰ συμφιλεῖν ἐφύν.

3. "Œdipus at Colonos" (Οἰδίπους ἐπὶ Κολωνῷ). This piece exhibits the death and burial, or rather disappearance, of Œdipus. It is rich in description and flatteries addressed to the Athenian people. The words of Œdipus, when talking to his daughter, are almost always very touching.

4. "Electra." This is the drama of "Orestes," given by Æschylus under a different name.

5. "Trachinia" (Τραχίνιαι). It is the death of Hercules, in which tragedy the chorus is composed of young females of Trachis.

6. "Ajax Armed with the Lash" (Αἴας μαστιγοφόρος). The subject of this piece is the madness of Ajax, his death, and the dispute which arises on the subject of his interment. It is a good piece.

7. "Philoctetes" (Φιλοκτήτης). We find in this play the mission of Ulysses to Philoctetes in the island of Lemnos, in order to induce him to come back to the Grecian army. He succeeded with great difficulty in accomplishing his object. This tragedy, although very simple in its plot, is marked by a constantly-increasing interest, and the characters are well supported. Sophocles, however, might have omitted several details at the beginning, which are hardly acceptable in poetry.

CΠAPTER III.

EURIPIDES AND THE LAST TRAGIC WRITERS OF THIS PE-
RIOD—THE THEATRE.

Euripides, the son of Mnesarchus and Clito, was
born in 480, at Phylæ, near Athens, on the day of the
battle of Salamis. The parents of Euripides must have
been of high standing, since Euripides was chosen to
discharge the office of cup-bearer in the festival of the
Delian Apollo. We read in Athenæus:

Οἰνοχόουν τε παρὰ τοῖς ἀρχαίοις οἱ εὐγενέστατοι παῖδες.

As we see, such office was intrusted only to boys distinguished by their nobility.

The father of Euripides directed in early life the
attention of his son to gymnastic exercises, and Euripides was crowned when he was but seventeen years
old in the Eleusinian contest. In acting thus, the father was determined by an oracle given him while his
wife was pregnant of the future dramatist. We read
in Aulus Gellius:

ἐς κλέος ἐσθλὸν ὀρούσει
καὶ στεφέων ἱερῶν γλυκερὴν χάριν ἀμφιβαλεῖται.

Euripides had a very stormy life. At the age of twenty
he became a painter; but, feeling that he was born a
poet, at a very early age also he was writing verses.
Few men have been more calumniated. Euripides
shared the fate common to all great men at Athens:
he went into exile, and found hospitality at the court

of Archelaus, King of Macedonia. There he provoked the envy of two poets, and was killed by dogs at the age of seventy-five. The following epitaph, written anonymously, is found in the " Anthologia : "

Οὐ σὸν μνῆμα τόδ᾽ ἔστ᾽ Εὐριπίδη, ἀλλὰ σὺ τοῦδε,
Τῇ σῇ γὰρ δόξῃ μνῆμα τόδ᾽ ἀμπέχεται.

A cenotaph was erected to his memory at Athens, bearing the following inscription :

Μνῆμα μὲν Ἑλλὰς ἅπασ᾽ Εὐριπίδου, ὀστέα δ᾽ ἴσχει
Τῇ Μακεδῶν· ἡ γὰρ δέξατο τέρμα βίου.
Πατρὶς δ᾽ Ἑλλάδος Ἑλλὰς Ἀθῆναι· πλεῖστα δὲ Μούσας
Τέρψας, ἐκ πολλῶν καὶ τὸν ἔπαινον ἔχει.

Euripides wrote seventy-five dramas, others say ninety-two, and some authors pretend that he composed as many as one hundred and twenty, but only eighteen are extant.

Æschylus gives supernatural and wonderful characters ; Sophocles dignified and heroic, but still natural ones ; Euripides gives the romance of private, every-day life, and his tragedies are pictures of the manners of Athens, and are not exaggerated. He is blamed for having lowered the style of tragedy ; this may be accepted as true, although Aristotle says the contrary, but Aristotle is not impartial. Euripides, besides being a poet, was a good philosopher, and consequently had the warm sympathies of Aristotle. He is blamed also for having lowered the character of women ; this reproach is from Aristophanes, but is not deserved ; moreover, the pictures given by Euripides are true, and won for him the popularity of his hearers. It is said that he made the divinity interfere too frequently in his plots, but we should consider that Euripides had not, concerning the gods, the opinion of Sophocles and Æschylus. The gods, in his opinion, were little more than mere men.

His prologues are criticised; in this he may be blamed, for they were long, and rendered the plot monotonous. Euripides was an enemy of demagogues, and no wonder; many traces of his political views are found in " Hecuba," where he attacks democratic principles under the character of Ulysses, and in " Orestes." His philosophical doctrine is not as pure as that of Æschylus, for we find in his writings such principles as the following one:

'Η γλῶσσ' ὀμώμοχ', ἡ δὲ φρὴν ἀνωμὸτος·

making light of the sacredness of an oath. His choral odes and lyric pieces are the most tender and the sweetest of his compositions, and his monodies are unrivalled. Already, at his time, the chorus had lost much of its prestige and religious character.

The style of Euripides is, on the whole, not compressed enough; although it presents us with some very happily-drawn pictures and ingenious turns of language, it has neither the dignity and energy of Æschylus, nor the chaste grace of Sophocles. Euripides was evidently a forerunner of the new comedy, for which he has a real inclination. The following is a list of his dramas now extant, in the order of merit, according to, as we think, the best critics:

1. " Hecuba." The subject is the sacrifice of Polyxena to the manes of Achilles, and the vengeance of

Hecuba killing the murderer of her son Polydorus. In this play the resignation of Polyxena, and the affection of Hecuba's mother, are the best scenes. This play has been imitated by several of the moderns, especially by Racine, and Voltaire in his "Merope."

2. "Medæa" (*Μηδεία*). We have in this play the vengeance of Medæa upon the unfaithful Jason. She kills the children which she had by him. The simplicity and clearness of the action constitute the principal charm of the play.

3. "Hippolytus" (*Ἱππόλυτος Στεφανόφορος*). Phædra, the mother of Hippolytus, becomes enamored of her son by the resentment of Venus, and, unable to satisfy her passion, she dies and leaves to Theseus, her husband, the care of destroying his own son. The play is good, and has been imitated by Racine in his tragedy called "Phèdre."

4. "Iphigenia in Aulis" (*Ἰφιγένεια ἡ ἐν Αὐλίδι*), and

5. "Iphigenia in Tauris" (*Ἰφιγένεια ἡ ἐν Ταύριδι*), are two good dramas, of which the subjects are well known, and have been treated partly already by Æschylus and Sophocles. In this last tragedy the best scene is the one in which Iphigenia and Orestes, her brother, become known to each other.

6. "Supplices" (*Ἱκέτιδες*). The Argive females, prostrated at Eleusis before the temple of Ceres, beseech Theseus to avenge their husbands killed before Thebes. Instead of a prologue, we have in this play a prayer to Ceres by the mother of Theseus, which is beautiful.

7. "Ion." This play is remarkable on account of the difficulties of the plan. Ion was the son of Apollo

and Creusa. Apollo aims to put Ion in such a position that his mother, not knowing him, intends to poison him, and he, not knowing his mother, endeavors to kill her. There is much resemblance between this tragedy and the "Athalie" of Racine. The play is very interesting.

8. "Helena" (Ἐλένη). The action is carried on in the island of Paros. Menelaus recognizes Helena, who is kept in custody by the king. She is delivered by a goddess.

9. "Orestes" (Ὀρέστης). The subject of this drama is the judgment of Orestes, and, the decision given by Menelaus is so unexpected by Orestes, that Apollo intervenes and saves him. The drama is not well conducted, and the *dénoûment* is unexpected; but the speech of the defender of Orestes is beautiful.

10. "Phenissæ" (Φοινίσσαι). This drama contains the death of Eteocles and Polynices. The title comes from the Phœnician women who composed the chorus. Grotius considers this play as the *chef-d'œuvre* of Euripides, but his opinion has not been accepted as the true one. There are several beauties, like the prologue presented by Jocasta.

11. "Alcestis." It is a melodrama, the subject of which is the death of Alcestis, in order to prolong her husband's life, and her rescue from hell by Hercules. On the whole, it is a feeble production.

12. "Andromache" (Ἀνδρομάχη). The subject is the death of the son of Achilles, whom Orestes slays, after having carried off from him Hermione. Racine has a piece of that name, but better composed. The "Andromache" of Euripides does not appear to us in

his piece, as we have known her while she was the wife of Hector.

13. " Troades (*Τρῶαδες*), or the Female Trojans." This piece describes the distribution of the captive matrons of Troy among the Greeks. The scene is laid in the Grecian camp, under the walls of Troy. There are some fine passages; Hecuba especially is beautiful.

14. " Bacchæ" (*Βάκχαι*). The arrival of Hercules at Thebes, and the death of Pentheus, torn from his mother and sister, form the subject of this play. The action is defective, having neither unity nor connection.

15. In the " Heraclidæ" the descendants of Hercules, being persecuted, ask for aid from Athens. There is much to interest in the piece.

16. " Hercules Furens" (*Ἡρακλῆς μαινόμενος*). After having killed his wife and children, Hercules proceeds to submit himself to certain expiatory ceremonies. The scene is laid at Thebes.

17. " Electra" (*Ἠλέκτρα*). The subject of this piece has been already treated by Sophocles under the same name. Euripides is inferior to Sophocles; however, he has succeeded in embellishing it with interesting episodes.

18. " Cyclops" (*Κύκλωψ*). It is a satyric drama, but not a comic, for the satyric drama is always tragic among the Greeks. The subject, which is taken from the " Odyssey," is Ulysses depriving Polyphemus of his eye, after having intoxicated him with wine. This piece contains many beautiful passages. The description of the character of the satyrs is very well given.

The piece called " Rhesus" was never written by

Euripides, but we have from him eighty verses remaining of a tragedy called "Phaeton."

We must add to the list of the dramatic poets the following names:

Ion.—He was born in Chios, and wrote from twelve to forty tragedies, but Bentley could collect only the titles of eleven and some fragments. These are too few to form an estimate of the author.

Achæus, born at Electria, in 484, exhibited from twenty-four to forty-four tragedies. Once he won a prize, and he had for competitors Sophocles and Euripides. Some fragments, and seventeen titles, are extant of his works.

Agathon was a native of Athens, and won the prize for the first time in 416. The most celebrated of his works bore the title of Ἄνθος (flower). We have the titles of four of his tragedies. Agathon was a great friend of Euripides.

A taste and talent for poetry continued for some time in the families of the three great dramatic poets, but it was only a profession, and no longer the result of inspiration.

Two names are found in the Alexandrian canon besides those already given: they are Chæremon and Theodectes. This last one wrote fifty tragedies, and once won the prize in the dramatic contest. We have some fragments of his works, but the writings of Chæremon are lost.

NOTE.—The theatre among the Greeks was not exactly on the same plan that is found later, especially in our time. It was disposed like an amphitheatre, having seats coming down on one side, and the stage facing them. It was in the open air, and the

CHAPTER IV.

COMEDY.

COMEDY took its origin from the Phallic song and the dithyrambic chorus. This origin shows sufficiently that it was at the beginning very low and licentious. Comedy is of Sicilian origin, but it soon flourished in

one of Athens, built on the slope of the Acropolis, could contain thirty thousand people. Among the seats some were reserved for the magistracy (βουλή), and formed the part called βουλευτικόν. The part called ἐφηβικόν contained the seats for the young men (ἔφηβοι), and the stage had in the front the orchestra. The stage itself extended forward in the orchestra, forming a sort of triangle, and the upper angle was the θυμέλη (thymele). It was the place where the chorus stood when not performing its solemn dance and song, and the leader of the chorus took his stand there when joining in the dialogue on the stage. The thymele was ornamented with an altar sacred to Dionysus, and therefore symbolical of the religious object of the spectacle.

The front part of the stage was called λογεῖον—because the actors stood there while speaking—and the back προσκήνιον. In each of these parts there were two entrances, or coulisses, one on each side. Under the orchestra were the stairs of Charon, whence the dead arose when there was in the piece any evocation from the infernal regions. In the centre there was the royal doorway (βασίλειον), whence the principal character of the play always made his entrance. The scenery was almost entirely architectural, but the ancients had also, when necessary, landscape painting. This part of the decoration was imperfect among them, and deprived their theatre of those effects of perspective which make ours so interesting. The actors were helped, in order to be seen and heard, by cothurns and masks.

In the back part of the theatre was the encyclema (ἐκκύκλημα), for representing scenes which could not be acted before the spec-

Attica, and there reached perfection. The authors assign generally three periods to the history of comedy: the first is the old one, or the period of Aristophanes, going as far as the ninety-eighth Olympiad; the characteristic of the old comedy is personality. From the ninety-eighth Olympiad to the one hundred and twelfth, when Philemon and Menander commence to exhibit, we have the second period, which is usually termed the Latin period—it is the period of Plautus and Terentius. The characteristic of the middle comedy is rather philosophical; it is an attack upon the follies of classes rather than of individuals. The third period com-

tators. The encyclema was a contrivance peculiar to the Greek stage. It was a semicircular machine, representing an interior, and, when the great central doors were thrown open, it was exposed to view, or, as some think, wheeled forward through the opening. The following instances are cited by Müller—from the tragedies of Æschylus, Sophocles, and Euripides—in which the encyclema was evidently employed:

ÆSCHYLUS.

1. In the "Agamemnon," v. 1345, the encyclema represented the apartment containing the bath, the murdered hero, and Clytemnestra, with the weapon in her hand reeking with blood.

2. In the "Chœphori," v. 967. The chamber as before; Orestes standing over the corpses of Clytemnestra and Ægisthus.

SOPHOCLES.

3. In the "Electra," v. 1450, a covered corpse is rolled upon the stage in an encyclema, which Ægisthus supposes to be Orestes. He unveils it, and behold it is Clytemnestra!

4. In the "Antigone," v. 1293. The corpse of Eurydice is thus exhibited after her suicide.

5. In the "Ajax," v. 346. The interior of the tent is thus thrown open to the view of the assembled people.

6. In the "Œdipus Tyrannus," v. 1297, the self-blinded mon-

menced after those authors, and resembles the one of our time. It is the comedy of manners which we have now, and is only the perfection of the comedy of the second period. It is in the pieces of Aristophanes that we may study the characteristic of the old comedy, he being the only writer from whom we have complete pieces. The old comedy does not resemble the comedy of the third period. The structure is loose and unconnected, the plot is incomplete and not uniform, and resembles rather a modern pantomime. It is a union of independent scenes and ludicrous situations, satirical attacks on the vices, and allusions to the follies of the

arch is thus shown for the first time after his terrible catastrophe.

EURIPIDES.

7. In the "Hercules Furens," v. 1030, Hercules is thus discovered bound to a pillar, and surrounded by the dead bodies of his wife and children.

8. In the "Hippolytus," v. 818, the doors of the palace are thrown open, and the corpse of Phædra is seen after her suicide.

The thymele was sometimes decorated in a more gorgeous way, when solemn sacrifices had to be offered, and then the chorus was in the orchestra.

The representations were given during the months of Poseidon, Gamelion, Anthesterion, and Elaphebolion; they were the sixth, seventh, eighth, and ninth months of the Athenians, that is, December, January, February, and March. The price of admission was two oboli (three and a quarter pence, or about seven cents). This formed the theoric fund, which was a sacred deposit.

The state gave to the poets fifty actors, that is, forty-eight choristers and two actors. The chorus was divided into two parts. They entered in files and ranks, marching three abreast. There were never more than three actors.

day. The humor consists principally in practical jokes;
it also indulged in the most unrestrained personalities.
This last character went so far that a law, passed in
440, forbade the poets to indulge in personalities; but
this law was abrogated by Alcibiades in 415. Such
representations, of course, were pleasing to the fickle-
minded public of Athens.

The old comedy was to the Athenian the representative of many influences which exist in the present
day; it was the newspaper, the review, the satire, the
pamphlet, the caricature, the pantomime of Athens.

Addressed to the thousands who flocked to the
theatre to witness the representation of a new comedy,
most of whom were keenly alive to every witty allusion and stroke of satire, and who took a deep interest
in every thing of a public nature—because each individual was personally engaged in the administration
of state affairs—the old comedy must have been a powerful engine for good or for evil. The comic poets indulged in the use of the Parabasis, a sort of mono-
logue, often out of the subject.

The first writer of comedies was Susarion, living at
the time of Solon, and born at Megara. Like Thespis,
he was accustomed to go with his theatre from one
place to another. Horace alludes to that custom when
he says:

"Ignotum tragicæ genus invenisse camenæ
    Dicitur, et plaustris vexisse poemata Thespis."

The following are the names of the first Sicilian
comic writers:

Epicharmus—who was the first of one hundred and

four comic writers, of whom Posidippus was the last, during a period of two hundred and fifty years—was born at Cos, in 540, but he performed at Megara, Sicily, and died at the age of ninety-seven. He composed thirty-five comedies, but scarcely more than the titles have been preserved. He was distinguished for elegance of composition, as well as originality of conception. Aristotle reproached him with the employment of false antitheses. So many were his dramatic excellences, that Plato terms him the first of comic writers. The plays of Epicharmus, to judge from the fragments still left us, abound with apophthegms little consistent with the idea we might otherwise have entertained of their nature from our knowledge of the buffooneries whence comedy sprung; but Epicharmus was a philosopher and a Pythagorean.

Phormis, a contemporary of Epicharmus, lived in Sicily. We have from him the titles of eight comedies.

Dinolochus, a Dorian comic writer, from Agrigentum, wrote fourteen comedies, and we have the titles of some of them.

Among the writers of the old Attic period we may give the following:

Chionides, from Athens, exhibited eight years before the Persian War, and composed nine plays, which are lost; but we may judge from the titles that they had a political tendency.

Cratinus, born in Attica, in 519, was represented as a genial fellow, fond of wine, and distinguished by the bitterness of his satires. None of his thirty-eight comedies remain, but we have the titles.

Eupolis (446), a native of Athens, was distinguished

for his broad humor and drollery, and also for the in-genuity of his double meaning. We have from him the titles of twenty comedies, and some fragments.

Crates lived in the time of Cratinus. His plays were remarkable also for broad humor and drollery We have the titles of eight out of his fourteen plays. According to Aristotle, he was the first Athenian poet who abandoned the iambic, or satyric, form of comedy, and made use of general stories or fables. Very likely the law alluded to above, and passed in 440, restrain-ing the virulence and license of comedy, had some share in giving his plays this less offensive turn. His style is said to have been gay and facetious, yet the few frag-ments of his writings which remain are of a serious cast.

Aristophanes, the prince of the old comedy, was born about 444, and probably at Athens. His father, Phi-lippus, had possessions in Ægina. Aristophanes ex-hibited for the first time in 427; he was very popular, but of his private history we know nothing. He prob-ably died at the age of seventy-six, having written fifty-four plays, of which eleven are extant. The fol-lowing epigram is found in the "Anthologia:"

Αἱ Χάριτες τέμενός τι λαβεῖν, ὅπερ οὐχὶ πεσεῖται
Ζητοῦσαι, ψυχὴν εὗρον Ἀριστοφάνους.

The titles of his plays are as follows:

1. "The Banqueters." The poet shows in this piece that gymnastic exercises would be advantageous to the health of the people; those exercises formed a part of the old education.

2. "The Acharnians." When the poet paints the sad evils of war, it was against the policy of Pericles.

3. "The Knights." This is an attack against demagogues, and a beautiful and true picture of the vices and follies of the Athenians is given herein.

4. "The Wasps." The object of this comedy is to attack the well-known litigiousness of the Athenian people.

5. "The Peace." As in the "Acharnians," the poet shows the miseries and privations attendant upon a long-protracted war.

6. "Lysistrata;" 7. "Thesmophoriazusæ;" 8. "Ecclesiazuæ." In these three plays, which are the coarsest of Aristophanes's dramas, we have a picture of the vices prevalent among the female sex.

9. "The Birds." In this play Aristophanes pretends to say that there was no remedy for the corrupt state of Athenian society, except in an entire restoration of the social system.

10. "Plutus" is a satiric essay upon the danger of riches.

11. "The Frogs" continues the attack upon the Euripidean tragedy, which was begun in the "Thesmophoriazusæ."

All the great tragic poets were now dead, and Greek tragedy had arrived at its period of decay. Dionysus, therefore, the god of tragedy, descends to the infernal regions in search of a poet. Æschylus and Euripides contend for the honor of returning to earth. A most amusing contest ensues, in which the peculiar merits and defects of each poet are exhibited, compared, and criticised. The question is for a long time undecided, but, at last, Euripides is ruined by his dishonest sophistry. He suffers a double defeat, for not only is

Æschylus selected to return to earth, but Sophocles is, during his absence, installed in the tragic throne below.

The comedy of "The Frogs" is distinguished for the beauty of its choral odes. These sweet and graceful poems satisfactorily prove that, while the author of them surpassed in wit all those writers who were eminent in his own walk of literature, he equalled in elegance of language and lyric talent the tragic poets themselves.

12. "The Clouds" is the most important of the tragedies of Aristophanes. In it the modern school of subtle and sophistical philosophy was the object of the poet's attack. The philosophy of the day was represented by Socrates. In looking about for a type of the philosopher, Aristophanes naturally fixed upon the one who attracted the largest share of public attention; who, from the tenor of his life and teaching, had made himself the greatest number of enemies; and who, for his eccentricities, laid himself most open to comic ridicule. Socrates was the most notorious of all who professed to be public instructors. Besides, he was an admirable subject for caricature; his ugly face, which was even copied in pottery and earthenware, his absent manners, his wild stare to the right and left as he walked, his bare feet and careless dress, and disregard of the common practices of Athenian polite life, pointed him out as the very man to represent the professors of that μετεωροσοφία, or soaring wisdom, which disdains the common concerns of life.

The comedy of "The Banqueters," which is spoken of first, does not exist any more, but we have many quotations and fragments from it. It is to be regretted that some of the comedies of Aristophanes are so lewd that we cannot with decency read them.

CHAPTER V.

PROSE—HISTORY—HERODOTUS.

WHILE the Greeks were cultivating poetry, the Semitic races—Egyptian, Assyrian, Hebrew—had historical records. The reason is that they were constituted generally in large monarchies, and their rulers had an interest in keeping the records of their glorious deeds. Greece had really no history before Herodotus, who has been called the Father of History.

Four historians, who came before him, have mixed history with legend. Many fragments remain from those historians, which have been collected by several German Hellenists, such as Clausen, Sturz, and Creuzer.

Pherecydes, of Leros, a small island near Miletus, flourished during the Persian War, and lived eighty-five years. He gave ten books of family records of Athens. He was much consulted by the later mythographers, and his numerous fragments must still serve as the basis of many mythological inquiries.

Charon was born at Lampsacus, a Milesian colony. He wrote a history of the Persian War, but he was a chronicler rather than an historian. Those early historians have been called also Horographers (Ὡρογράφοι), as it were, giving an account hour by hour.

Hellanicus, of Mitylene, in the island of Lesbos, was almost a contemporary of Herodotus. He wrote numerous works in the way of chronicles, but nothing complete remains. According to Thucydides, and several writers who do not belong to the classical period, *il n'a pas de critique.* Some, however, pretend that he was a learned and diligent compiler, and that, so far as his sources went, he was a trustworthy one. He lived eighty-five years.

Xanthus was a native of Sardis (Lydia). This point, however, is a doubtful one, as also the period when he flourished. Xanthus wrote a history of Lydia, of which some considerable fragments have come down to us.

HERODOTUS.

Herodotus was born at Halicarnassus, in 484. His family, which was one of the most distinguished in the

4

city, was exposed to the persecution of the tyrant Lyg-damis. Herodotus, at a very early age, had to fly to Samos. There he cultivated the Ionic dialect, and there, too, imbibed the Ionic spirit which pervades his history. He joined in an attempt which was made in order to free Samos from the tyranny of Lygdamis. The at-tempt proved successful, but soon after Herodotus again left his country and settled in Magna Græcia, at Thurii. It is there, very likely, that he wrote his work, that he died at a very old age, and was buried.

Herodotus presents himself to our consideration in three points of view—as a traveller, an observer, and an historian. The extent of his travels may be ascertained pretty clearly from his history ; but the order in which he visited each place, and the time of visiting, cannot be determined. His travels, however, must have occu-pied a considerable period of his life, and he would seem to have first entered upon them in the full strength of body and mind, and after having been completely educated.

The history of his reading his work at the Olympic games, which has found its way into most modern nar-ratives, has been ably discussed, and, it may be said, has been disproved.

With a simplicity which characterizes his whole work, Herodotus makes no display of the great extent of his travels ; and he is so free from the ordinary vanity of travellers, that, instead of acting a prominent part in his narrative, he very seldom appears at all in it. Hence, it is impossible to give any thing like an accu-rate chronological succession of his travels. In Greece proper, or on the coasts of Asia Minor, there is scarcely any place of importance with which he is not perfectly familiar from his own observation, and where he did not make inquiries respecting this or that particular point; we may mention more especially the oracular places, such as Dodona and Delphi. He also visited most of the Greek islands.

As for his travels in foreign countries, we know that he sailed through the Hellespont, the Propontis, and crossed the Euxine in both directions. With the Palus Mæotis he was imperfectly acquainted. He further visited Thrace and Scythia. The interior of Asia Minor was well known to him, especially Lydia, and so was also Phœnicia. He visited Tyre for the special purpose of obtaining information respecting the worship of Hercules. Previous to this he had been in Egypt, for it was in Egypt that his curiosity respecting Hercules had been excited.

A second source from which Herodotus drew his information was the literature of his country, especially the poetical portion, for prose had not yet been cultivated very extensively, as we have just had occasion to observe. With the poems of Homer and Hesiod he was perfectly familiar, though he attributed less historical importance to them than might have been expected. He was also acquainted with the poetry of Alcæus, Sappho, Simonides, Pindar, and Æschylus.

The object of the work of Herodotus is to give an account of the struggles between the Greeks and Persians, from which the former, with the help of the Ionians, came off victorious. He traces the enmity between Europe and Asia to the mythical times. But he rapidly passes over the mythical ages to come to

Crœsus, King of Lydia, who was known to have committed acts of hostility against the Greeks; this induces him to give a full history of Crœsus and the kingdom of Lydia. The conquest of Lydia by the Persians, under Cyrus, then leads him to relate the rise of the Persian monarchy, and the subjugation of Asia Minor and Babylon. The history of Cambyses, and his expedition into Egypt, induce him to enter into the details of Egyptian history. The expedition of Darius against the Scythians, causes him to speak of Scythia and the north of Europe. The kingdom of Persia now extended from Scythia to Cyrene, and, an army being called in by the Cyreneans against the Persians, Herodotus proceeds to give an account of Cyrene and Libya. In the mean time the revolt of the Ionians broke out, which eventually brings the contest between Persia and Greece to an end. An account of this insurrection, and of the rise of Athens after the expulsion of the Pisistratidæ, is followed by what properly constitutes the principal part of the work, and the history of the Persian War now runs on ‚ in a regular channel until the taking of Sestos.

The great structure of the history thus bears a strong resemblance to a grand epic poem. The work, however, has an abrupt termination, and is probably incomplete. The division of the history into nine books, each bearing the name of a muse, was made by some grammarian, for there is no indication in the whole composition of the divisions having been made by the author himself. The entire work is pervaded by a profoundly religious idea, which distinguishes Herodotus from all other Greek historians. In order to form a fair judgment of the historical value of the work of Herodotus, we must distinguish those parts in which he speaks from his own observation, or gives the results of his own investigations, from those in which he merely repeats what he was told by priests, interpreters, guides, and the like. In the latter case, he was undoubtedly often deceived; but he never intrudes such reports as any thing more than they really are, and, under the influence of his natural good sense, he frequently cautions his reader by some such remarks as—"I know this only from hearsay;" or, "I have been told so, but do not believe it." But, whenever he speaks from his own observation, Herodotus is a real model of truthfulness and accuracy, and the more those countries of which he speaks have been explored by modern travellers, the more firmly has his authority been established.

The dialect in which Herodotus wrote is the Ionic, intermixed with epic or poetical expressions, and sometimes even with Attic and Doric forms. This peculiarity of his language called forth a number of lexicographical words of learned grammarians, all of which are lost, with the exception of a few remnants in the Homeric glosses. The excellences of his style do not consist in any artistic or melodious structure of his sentences, but in the antique and epic coloring, the transparent clearness, the lively flow of his narrative, and his natural and unaffected gracefulness. There is, perhaps, no work in the whole range of ancient literature which so closely resembles a familiar and homely oral narration as that of Herodotus. Its reader cannot help feeling as though he were listening to an old man, who, from the inexhaustible stores of his knowledge and experience, tells his stories with that single-hearted simplicity and *naïveté*, which are the marks and indications of a truthful spirit.

CHAPTER VI.

HISTORY—THUCYDIDES—XENOPHON—CTESIAS.

Thucydides is the inventor of philosophical history. He was born at Halimus, near Athens, in 471, and was the son of Olonus and Hegesipyle. Lucian says that Thucydides was present when, at the Olympian games, Herodotus read his history before the assembled Greeks, and that he shed tears; but this is a fable, very likely, as well as the incident of Herodotus reading his history under such circumstances. It is said that Thucydides was instructed in oratory by Antiphon, and in philosophy by Anaxagoras. We have no trustworthy evidence of Thucydides having distinguished himself as an orator, though from his speeches we may conclude that he possessed an oratorical talent. He was, however, employed in a military capacity, and was in command of the Athenian fleet at Thasos, in 424, when he was sent to Amphipolis in order to protect that city against Brasidas, a Spartan general. He arrived too late, and was on that account exiled. It is not known where he went to, but evidently he did not go to any place which was under Athenian dominion. It is very likely that, during the time of his exile, he collected materials and wrote his work. The exile of Thucydides lasted twenty years. He may have returned to Athens, in 403, and, according to some very reliable accounts, he was assassinated.

With Thucydides history is solid instruction; its incidents convey lessons for statesmen, as well as for individuals in any state of life. The example of Thucydides has been followed in modern times, but it is a

THUCYDIDES.

question whether there has been any who has surpassed him, for thoughtfulness and suggestiveness. Thucydides wrote "The Peloponnesian War;" he gave only twenty-one years of that war. It has been thought that the eighth book was not from him, because there is no speech in it. This reason is a weak one; the slight difference which exists between that book and the other ones, allows us only to conclude that Thucyd-

ides had no time to revise it. For that book cannot
be the work of the continuators of Thucydides; neither
is it by Xenophon, who took other divisions in his narration; nor by Theopompus, whose style is quite different from that of Thucydides. This writer opens his
work with a beautiful sketch of Greek history. The
war was a war of races—a contest between the Dorian
and the Ionian races. Thucydides, though an Ionian,
is impartial. It was also a contest between aristocratic
Athens and demagogic Sparta. Thucydides was a par-
tisan of aristocracy. He knew by experience whither
the mob could lead a government. The authority of
Thucydides was, of course, very great. The speeches
form the most prominent part of the work. Cicero crit-
icises them for their difficulty and obscurity, but Aristotle praises them, saying, with reason, that Thucydides did not write his book in order to satisfy the curiosity of the present age, but for the instruction of posterity; besides, there was as yet no treatise on the art
of speaking (oratory). The speeches were characteristic: laconic on the side of the Spartans, poetic on
the side of the Athenians. Throughout the whole
work there is a strict love of truth; descriptions are
avoided. The qualities in which Thucydides has seldom been equalled are moral wisdom and political
sagacity. The episode of the Corcyrian War, in which
he points out the causes of the sedition, is very good.
Thucydides confined himself strictly to his subject. In
recapitulation these two historians are very good.

Xenophon, the son of Gryllus, was born at Athens,
in 444. He was a soldier in his youth, and saved by
Socrates at the battle of Delium (424). At the insti-

gation of Proxenus, he joined the expedition of Cyrus the Younger against Artaxerxes Mnemon. After the defeat of Cyrus in the plain of Cunaxa, he retreated, with ten thousand Greeks, and, after fifteen months, they arrived at Trapezus (Trebizond), being eight thousand five hundred in number. Xenophon could never return to Athens; a decree had been issued against him, and he was banished for two reasons—he was a friend of Socrates, and a friend of Sparta. Agesilaus was with Xenophon during the Asiatic expedition; he was recalled to Greece, and Xenophon accompanied him to Sparta, and accepted from that king a country-seat, near Scyllus, where he spent a long time, hunting, entertaining his friends, writing some of his works —in one word, living like a gentleman. It is not known how, when, or where he died.

The extant works of Xenophon may be divided into four classes: 1. Historical, comprising "The Anabasis," "The Hellenica," "The Cyropædia," and "The Life of Agesilaus;" 2. Didactic, comprising "The Hipparchicus," the "Treatise on Horsemanship," and that on "Hunting;" 3. Political, comprising the works on the republics of Sparta and Athens, and "The Revenues of Athens;" 4. Philosophical, comprising "The Memorabilia of Socrates," "The Œconomicus," "The Symposium, or Banquet," "The Hiero," and "The Apology of Socrates."

There are also extant certain letters attributed to Xenophon, but, like many other ancient productions of the same class, they are not genuine.

1. HISTORICAL WORKS.—"The Anabasis" ('Aνάβα-σις), in seven books, is the work by which Xenophon

is best known. The first book gives the march of Cyrus to the neighborhood of Babylon, and ends with his death. The last six books contain the account of the retreat of the ten thousand. The work is written in an easy, agreeable style, and gives a great deal of curious information respecting the country traversed by the Greeks, and the manners of the people. It is full of interest also as being a minute detail by an eye-witness of the hazards and adventures of the army in their difficult march through an unknown and hostile country.

"The Hellenica" (Ἑλληνικά) is a Greek history, divided into seven books, and comprising the space of forty-eight years, from the time when the history of Thucydides ends to the battle of Mantinea (362). This book has little merit as a history, for Xenophon does not give the philosophy of the events which he relates like Thucydides. It is in general a dry narration, and contains little to move or affect, with the exception of a few incidents better narrated.

"The Cyropædia" (Κύρου παιδεία), in eight books, is a kind of political romance, in which the ethical element prevails; but, since it is based upon the history of Cyrus the Elder, it is commonly ranked among the historical works of Xenophon. Its object is to show how citizens can be formed to be virtuous and brave, and to exhibit also a model of a wise and good governor. It is an agreeable exposition of principles under the form of a history. The dying speech of Cyrus is worthy of a pupil of Socrates.

"The Agesilaus" (Ἀγησίλαος) is a panegyric of Xenophon's friend, the Lacedæmonian king, and forms another proof of his Spartan predilections. It is a kind of composition in which failure can hardly be avoided.

2. DIDACTIC WORKS.—"The Hipparchicus" ('Ιπ-παρχικός) is a treatise on the duties of a commander of cavalry, and contains many military precepts, especially for the choice of cavalrymen.

The "Treatise on Horsemanship" ('Ιππική) was written after "The Hipparchicus."

"The Cynegeticus" (Κυνηγετικός) is a treatise on hunting, an amusement of which Xenophon was very fond; and on the dog, and the breeding and training of dogs, on the various kinds of game, and the mode of taking them.

3. POLITICAL WORKS.—Two treatises on "The Republics of Sparta and of Athens" (Λακεδαιμονίων Πολιτεία, 'Αθηναίων Πολιτεία). The writer clearly prefers the Spartan to the Athenian institutions.

4. PHILOSOPHICAL WORKS.—"The Memorabilia of Socrates" ('Απομνημονεύματα Σωκράτους), in four books, contains a defence of the memory of Socrates against the charge of irreligion, and of corrupting the Athenian youth. Socrates is represented as holding a series of conversations, in which he develops and inculcates moral doctrines in his peculiar fashion. It is entirely a practical work, such as we might expect from the practical nature of Xenophon's mind, and it professes to exhibit Socrates as he taught. It is true that it may exhibit only one side of the Socratic argumentation, and that it does not deal in those subtleties and verbal disputes which occupy so large a space in some of Plato's dialogues. In "The Memorabilia" we have

as genuine a picture of Socrates as his pupil Xenophon could exhibit.

"The Œconomicus" (Οἰκονομικός) is a dialogue
between Socrates and Critobolus, in which Socrates
begins by showing that there is an art called Œconomy
(Οἰκονομική), which relates to the administration of a
household, and of a man's property. Cicero copied
some passages of this book in his treatise on "Old
Age." The seventh chapter is on the duty of a good
wife. This is one of the best treatises of Xenophon.

"The Symposium (Συμπόσιον), or Banquet of Philosophers," contains a delineation of the character of
Socrates. The speakers are supposed to meet at the
house of Callias, a rich Athenian, at the celebration
of the great Panathenæa. Socrates, Critobulus, Antisthenes, Charmides, and others, are the speakers. The
accessories of the entertainment are managed with
skill, and the piece is interesting as a picture of an
Athenian drinking-party, and of the amusement and
conversation with which it was diversified.

"The Hiero" (Ἱέρων ἢ Τύραννος) is a dialogue between King Hiero and Simonides, in which the king
speaks of the dangers and difficulties incident to an
exalted station, and the superior happiness of a private man.

"The Apology of Socrates" (Ἀπολογία Σωκράτους
πρὸς τοὺς δικαστάς) is not, as the title imports, the defence which Socrates made on his trial, but it contains
the reasons which determined him to prefer death,
rather than to humble himself by asking for his life
from his prejudiced judges. This treatise is inferior
in style and composition to all the other works of Xeno-

phon, and some have supposed, on that account, that it was not from him; but Diogenes Laërtius says positively that Xenophon wrote that apology, and that testimony should be sufficient.

Xenophon was an accomplished man. As a writer he deserves praise for perspicuity and ease, and for these qualities he has in all ages been justly admired. As an historical writer he is much below Thucydides. He had no depth of reflection, and no great insight into the fundamental principles of society. Xenophon was too business-like to be a poet, too much a citizen of the world to be a patriot, and too practical to be a deep philosopher. In order to complete the list of the historical writers of the classical period of Greek literature, we must give the names of—

1. **Ctesias,** who was a contemporary of Xenophon, and lived as a private physician at the court of Artaxerxes Mnemon, and, having a free access to the library of the palace, he collected materials for a history of Persia, and of India, of which works we have but fragments. He composed, besides those two books of history, three other works, of which we know little more than the titles.

2. **Philistus,** a Syracusan, was one of the most celebrated historians of antiquity, though unfortunately only a few fragments of his works have come down to us. He wrote a complete history of Sicily.

3. **Theopompus,** of Chios, a celebrated Greek historian, was born in 378. The titles of his works, none of which have come down to us, are an "Epitome of the History of Herodotus," a "History of Greece," "The History of Philip," and many orations.

4. **Ephorus,** who was a contemporary of Philip and Alexander, flourished in 340, and was a native of Cumæ, in Æolis. The most celebrated of the works of Ephorus was a "General History," in thirty books; we have also some fragments.

We have only fragments of the writings of the historians of Alexander the Great, who followed in the train of the monarch, or who were his companions in arms. These were: Anaximenes, Callisthenes, Clitarchus, Ptolemæus, Aristobulus, Onesicritus, Nearchus, Chares, Ephippus, Marsyas, Androsthenes, and Medius.

CHAPTER VII.

PROSE—ELOQUENCE.

ELOQUENCE is one of the principal characteristics of Greek literature, whether poetical, historical, or philosophical. The heroes of Homer are all orators. The very philosophers, who despised eloquence and were the rivals of the orators, could not help being eloquent; and Cicero observes that, what he most admired on reading "Gorgias" was, that Plato, while deriding orators, showed himself the most consummate and accomplished orator of them all. Eloquence gives a charm to the writings of Herodotus, Thucydides, and Xenophon. But Greek eloquence, in its perfection, owes a large debt of gratitude to Thucydides. It is true that Cicero denies that any rhetorician drew the principles of his art from the speeches of Thucydides, but the Roman orator is mistaken in this case.

Although the Greeks were by nature orators, as they were poets, oratory as an art is of Sicilian origin. The first treatises (τέχνη ρετορική) were written in Sicily by Corax, Tisias, and especially Gorgias, in the middle of the fifth century before Christ. The writings of these rhetors are lost. Gorgias transported that art to Athens, where a school was soon established, and Alcibiades was one of the first disciples of Gorgias. A great rivalry existed at the beginning between the Sophists, who were then the most celebrated teachers, and the Philosophers.

Oratory appears to have been much abused during the Peloponnesian War. We may, among the orators of that period, who were really distinguished for their talents, give the names of Pericles, Alcibiades, and Cleophon. With such a public as the one composing the Ecclesia of Athens, it was difficult for an orator to be honest. Eloquence was so much abused at that time, that Aristophanes said that a scoundrel only could succeed as an orator. Whatever may be the truth of this assertion, we may judge by the rules given by Aristotle, and the remarks of Longinus about the orations of Demosthenes, that it was no less difficult to please the Athenian ear than to be honest. The orator had to be well prepared before appearing in public, and, in order to succeed, he was obliged to have quickness and tact in observing the state of feeling which pervaded the assembly, a comprehensive and retentive memory, a perfect knowledge of human nature, and of the resources of the Greek language, and a wide range of political and historical information.

Greek eloquence arose and flourished during the

period of Greek liberty.   It did not entirely decay until Athenian independence was utterly crushed. Both died together.   Freedom has always been favorable to oratory; it finds no place under tyranny and absolutism.   Hence, while eloquence flourished under the protection of Athenian democracy, Sparta never produced an orator.   The canon of Attic orators, as settled in a later age by the Alexandrian grammarians, contains ten names, given in chronological order, as follows :

Antiphon, born at Rhamnus in Attica, in 479, was a teacher of rhetoric and composer of orations.   The democratic party condemned him to death, on account of his oligarchical opinions.   Thucydides, a pupil of Antiphon, speaks of his master with the highest esteem, and many of the excellences of his style are ascribed by the ancients to the influence of Antiphon.   Antiphon, as we have said, composed speeches for others, who delivered them in the courts of justice, and, as he was the first who received money for such orations—a practice which subsequently became quite general—he was severely attacked and ridiculed.   The unpopularity which was the result of these attacks, together with his own reserved character, prevented his ever appearing as a speaker, either in the courts or in the assembly; and the only time he spoke in public was in 411, when, on the overthrow of the oligarchical government, Antiphon was brought to trial for having attempted to negotiate peace with Sparta, and was condemned to death.   His speech in defence of himself was the ablest which has ever been made by any man in similar circumstances.   Fifteen harangues are extant from the writings of Antiphon. They are of the kind (λόγοι φονικοί), having reference to criminal proceedings, and especially deserve attention as giving an idea of the way of proceeding in the Greek tribunals.*

Andocides was born at Athens, in 467. He was also persecuted by the democratic party, and banished from Athens. As an orator Andocides does not appear to have been held in very high esteem by the ancients, as he is seldom mentioned. We have three orations from him. Andocides, not having been trained in any of the sophistical schools of his time, his orations have no mannerism, but they are simple, and free from rhetorical pomp and ornament. Sometimes his style is diffuse, and becomes tedious and obscure. The best of his orations is the one on "The Mysteries" (περὶ τῶν Μυστηρίων), which he pronounced when his enemies accused him of having profaned them.

Lysias was born at Athens, in 458. He lived thirty-two years in the Athenian colony of Thurii, in Italy. He was exiled from that place by the Dorians, and returned to Athens. He was also banished from that city, some time after his arrival, by the thirty tyrants. Lysias then went to Megara, and, in 402, returned to Athens, where he died in 378, at the age of eighty. Lysias was one of the most fertile writers of orations that Athens ever produced, for there were in antiquity no less than four hundred and twenty-five orations which were current under his name. Of these orations

* Besides the λόγοι φονικοί the ancients had two other kinds of public orations—λόγοι δημογορικοί, or discourses pronounced in the assemblies of the people; and λόγοι δικανικοί, or judiciary discourses.

only thirty-five are extant, and even among these some are incomplete. We have fragments of fifty-three others. Most of these orations were composed after his return from Thurii. How highly the orations of Lysias were valued in antiquity, may be inferred from the great number of persons who wrote commentaries upon them. The diction of Lysias is perfectly pure; his language is natural and simple, but, at the same time, noble and dignified; it is always clear and lucid. The copiousness of his style does not injure its precision, nor can his rhetorical embellishments be considered as impairing the charming simplicity of his manner of expression. His delineations of character are always striking, and true to life. But what characterizes his orations above those of all other ancients, is the indescribable gracefulness and elegance which pervades all of them, without in the least impairing their power and energy.

Isocrates also was born at Athens, in 436. He was called the great master of eloquence. He founded a school of rhetoric, and the princes of eloquence were formed there. Isocrates took a proper view of the aim of eloquence, despised the subtleties of the Sophists, and applied ornaments in a just proportion. Isocrates was never a public man; he was naturally timid and of a weakly constitution, and, on that account, he abstained from taking any direct part in the political affairs of his country. He resolved to contribute toward the development of eloquence, by teaching and writing. He established his first school at Chios, and afterward transferred it to Athens. Isocrates killed himself after the battle of Chæronea, being ninety-nine years old.

The language of Isocrates is the most refined Attic, and thus formed a great contrast to the pure and natural simplicity of Lysias, as well as the sublime power of Demosthenes. His artificial style is more elegant than graceful, and more ostentatious than pleasing. The carefully-rounded periods, the frequent applications of figurative expressions, are features which remind us of the Sophists; and, although his sentences flow very melodiously, yet they become wearisome and monotonous by the perpetual recurrence of the same over-refined periods, which are not relieved by being interspersed with shorter and easier sentences. In saying this, however, we must remember that Isocrates wrote his orations to be read, and not with a view to their recitation before the people. We have from Isocrates twenty-one orations; eight of them belong to the kind λόγοι δικανικοί, five are λόγοι δημογορικοί, three are of a moral kind, and four are eulogies. The most remarkable is the discourse entitled " Panegyrical Oration " (Πανηγυρικός), a discourse which was intended to be pronounced before the assembled people.

Isæus was a native of Chalcis, or, as some say, of Athens. Very little is known about his life, although he established a rhetorical school at Athens, and Demosthenes is said to have been one of his pupils. Eleven orations are extant from Isæus. They are all on subjects connected with disputed inheritances, and Isæus appears to have been particularly well acquainted with the laws relating to inheritance. The oratory of Isæus resembles in many points that of his teacher, Lysias. The style of both is pure, clear, and concise.

Æschines, the son of Atrometus and Glaucothea,

was born in 389, and, in his youth, he appears to have assisted his father, who kept a small school; he next acted as secretary to Antiphon, then he tried his fortune as an actor, for which he was provided by Nature with a strong and sonorous voice. After this he left the stage and engaged in military services, in which, according to his own account, he gained great distinction. Æschines afterward came forward at Athens as a public speaker, and the military fame which he had now acquired established his reputation. During the first period of his public career Æschines was, like all other Athenians, zealously engaged in directing the attention of his fellow-citizens to the growing power of Philip, and exhorted them to check it in its growth. In 347 he was sent, along with Demosthenes, as one of the ten ambassadors to negotiate a peace with Philip. From this time he appears as the friend of the Macedonian party, and as the opponent of Demosthenes.

Æschines and Demosthenes were at the head of two parties, into which not only Athens but all Greece were divided, and their political enmity created and nourished perpetual hatred. The last great event in the public life of Æschines was his prosecution of Ctesiphon, in the question of the crown. When Æschines lost his cause, not having obtained one-fifth of the votes of the judges, he was then compelled to leave Athens, being unable to pay the penalty in that case required by the law. Æschines went to Asia Minor; he spent several years in Ionia and Caria, occupying himself with teaching rhetoric, and anxiously waiting for the return of Alexander to Europe. After the death of Alexander he returned to Rhodes, where probably he died. The conduct of Æschines has been censured by the writers of all ages; but it is impossible to arrive at the complete truth, from the perplexing history of a period, when the principal authorities are two political rivals, whose statements about the matter under consideration are often in direct contradiction to one another. But, if the integrity of Æschines is suspected, his great abilities both as a popular leader and an orator are undisputed; he was the rival, and, according to Cicero and Quintilian, all but the equal of Demosthenes. In the lucid arrangement of his matter, and in the ease and clearness of his narrative, he has never been surpassed; and, if he falls below Demosthenes in any quality of an orator, it is in powerful invective and vehement passion. The facility and felicity of his diction, the boldness and vigor of his descriptions, carry away his reader now, as they must have carried away his hearers in former times. We have only three orations from Æschines.

LYCURGUS.

Lycurgus, the namesake of the great Lacedæmonian

lawgiver, was born at Athens, in 396. He was a distinguished administrator, and he left the reputation of a very honest, unflinching character. The people loved him, and public honors were paid to him after his death. Of the fifteen orations of Lycurgus, which are mentioned by Plutarch, only one has come down to us. Diodorus of Sicily greatly praises Lycurgus's eloquence, but Dionysius of Halicarnassus says that he was deficient in ease and elegance. This judgment is true concerning the style of that orator.

Demosthenes, the greatest of the Greek orators, was the son of Demosthenes, and was born in the Attic borough of Pæania, in 385. He raised eloquence to the highest degree of style, reasoning, composition, skill, and vigor. The position of Demosthenes, when he had to interfere in the administration, was a difficult one. Athens had not to fight for its supremacy any more, but for its independence, and patriotism was extinct in some of the orators, especially in Æschines. They were sold to Philip. Demosthenes, on the contrary, showed himself a real patriot.

His father died when he was young, and his guardian took his property from him; but, by his talent, Demosthenes recovered a great part of it. Demosthenes studied eloquence with energy, we might say with heroism. The physical disadvantages under which he labored are well known, and the manner in which he surmounted them is often quoted as an example to encourage others to persevere. He was naturally of a weak constitution; he had a feeble voice, an indistinct articulation, and a shortness of breath. His first office was the one of Choregus, and, in the discharge of its functions, he manifested his talent for eloquence in the condemnation of Medias, who had assailed him. It was about the year 355 that Demosthenes began to obtain reputation as a speaker in the public assembly. It was by his eloquence that he prevented an expedition to Eubœa, and avoided a war with Persia. For

DEMOSTHENES.

fourteen years he struggled against Philip, and, when that prince attacked the northern cities of Greece allied to Athens, Demosthenes, in his three "Olynthiacs," discovered more plainly the plans of Philip; but he could not persuade the Athenians in time, and Olynth was taken. Philip then interfered openly in the affairs of Greece, and was appointed the chief of the Amphictyonic league. It was the last step toward invasion; Demosthenes pronounced at that time his last "Philippics." * The party of Philip, headed by Æschines, became stronger. It was at this time that the

* This name has been retained since as synonymous with invective discourses.

contest for the crown took place. After the death of
Philip, Alexander, with reluctance, allowed Demosthenes to remain at Athens. Having been accused
of accepting the bribes of Harpalus, he was exiled,
but recalled soon after. After the death of Alexander, hearing that Antipater was marching on Athens, he fled to the island of Calauria and poisoned
himself.

We have sixty orations from Demosthenes; besides
these orations we have fifty-six exordia ($Προοίμια$
$δημηγορικά$). His discourses are of three kinds: deliberative, judicial, and studied or show speeches ($λόγοι$
$ἐπιδεικτικοί$); seventeen belong to the first class, forty-
one to the second class, and two to the third. The
best are the twelve "Philippics," in which are included
the three "Olynthiacs;" these are deliberative discourses. The best in the judicial kind is the discourse
entitled "Concerning the Crown" ($Περὶ Στεφάνου$).
Demosthenes had been twice crowned in the theatre
during the Dionysiac festival. In the second year of
the one hundred and tenth Olympiad, Ctesiphon, who
was then president of the Senate, had a decree passed
by that body, that, if the people approved, Demosthenes should be crowned at the approaching Dionysiac festival, in the theatre, as a recompense for the
disinterested manner in which he had filled various
offices, and for the services which he had constantly
rendered the state; but, before this matter was brought
before the people for confirmation, Æschines presented
himself as the accuser of Ctesiphon. He charged him
with having violated the laws, in proposing to crown
a public functionary before the latter had given an ac-

count of the manner in which he had discharged his office, etc. He concluded by demanding that a fine of fifty talents be imposed upon Ctesiphon. On account of political difficulties, the affair remained for some time pending; but, eight years later, Æschines again brought forward his accusation. Æschines thereupon pronounced his famous harangue, to which Demosthenes replied. This speech of Demosthenes is regarded, and justly so, not only as his *chef-d'œuvre*, but as the most perfect specimen that eloquence has ever produced. Such is the opinion of Dionysius of Halicarnassus. Modern critics come to the same conclusion. The two discourses of the kind λόγοι ἐπιδείκτικοι (studied or set speeches) are evidently spurious. The one, ἐπιτάφιος λόγος, is an eloge on the Athenians who had perished at Chæronea; the other, ἐρώτικος λόγος, is written in praise of the beauty of the young Epicrates. Three things are found in the discourses of Demosthenes, which must have been the cause of the mighty impression made upon the minds of his hearers: 1. It was their pure and ethical character—each sentence exhibits Demosthenes as a true patriot; 2. It was his intellectual superiority—the subject is well arranged, the arguments are strong and properly disposed, and the objections clearly refuted; 3. It was the magic force of his language, which was at the same time majestic and simple, rich but not bombastic, strange and familiar, solemn but not too much ornamented, grave and yet pleasing, concise and fluent, sweet and impressive.

Hyperides, born at Athens, in 396, was a distinguished orator, and even may be compared with De-

5

mostheues.   There is more wit in his discourses.   He
also was a victim of political disasters, and was killed
by Antipater, at Ægina, where he fled after the battle
of Cranon (322).   Unfortuuately, we have no oration
from him.   Libanius, however, gives as one of his discourses one found among the orations of Demosthenes
(Περὶ τῶν πρὸς Ἀλεξανδρόν συνθηκῶν), concerning the
treaties with Alexander.

Dinarchus, a native of Corinth, where he was born
in 360.   He is the last of the ten orators composing
the Attic canon.   He went very early to Athens.   Evidently Dinarchus owes his celebrity to the decline of
the art.   He wrote one hundred and sixty discourses,
but we have only three extant from him.   Those three
discourses euable us to form an opinion upon the merits
of Dinarchus, and we find that the opinion expressed
above, when we observed that his celebrity is due to
the decline of the art, is quite correct.   It is difficult
to say whether Dinarchus had any oratorical talent or
not, for there is surely no originality of mind.

There was living at that time a man who was an
orator, but who may be considered as the shame of the
art of oratory at that period.   It was Demades, who
was venal, dishonest, and corrupt in his morals.   He
became an object of disgust to his friends themselves.
Antipater had him put to death in 319.

CHAPTER VIII.

PROSE—PHILOSOPHY.

WE have seen that philosophy, before Pericles, was more or less materialistic. Three divisions are found in it: 1. The school of Thales, denying the existence of a first cause, and admitting the eternity of matter; 2. The Pythagorean school, trying to explain the phenomena, either physical or metaphysical, by mathematical analogies, and not by some mechanical power as before—they admit the existence of a first cause; 3. The Eleatic school, which was a sort of eclectic school; it examined the views of its predecessors, and brought them to the test of logical principles. This school became spiritualistic. The philosophers who wrote immediately before the Socratic period, belonged rather to this school; among them are Leucippus and Democritus. This last philosopher wrote many books, which have been praised by Cicero for the beauty of their style, but only fragments have come down to us. The philosophers did not give a system which was sufficiently adequate; hence skepticism, under various forms, made its appearance, and was found at the bottom of the teachings of all those philosophers.

The Sophists then came, and laid aside the former systems. The starting-point of the sophistical philosophy was the famous maxim—Γνῶθι σεαυτόν. It was a good starting-point, since the former systems had failed to establish a reasonable system of philosophy. The Sophists are better known as the educators of the

youth at Athens, and they were accused of corrupting
their pupils.   To represent the Sophists as wilful and
designing impostors, whose object was to corrupt the
public morality, is going too far.   It is enough to say
that they professed to qualify the youth of the leading
families to shine, and become influential in a degener-
ate state of society; they did not think that they
should teach their pupils to aspire to higher and nobler
views.   A low moral standard was set up and admitted,
and they did not care to elevate it.   Still, this was not
general among the Sophists.

If, now, we turn from the influence of the Sophists
on the spirit of their age, and set ourselves to inquire
what they did for the improvement of written compositions, we are constrained to set a very high value on
their services.   The formation of an artificial prose
style is due entirely to the Sophists, and, although they
did not at first proceed according to a rigid method,
they may be considered as having laid a foundation for
the polished diction of Plato and Demosthenes.   The
Sophists of Greece proper, as well as those of Sicily,
made language the object of their study, but with this
distinction, that the former aimed at correctness, and
the latter at beauty of style.   The view here taken of
the Sophists is the one that is commonly entertained
respecting them.   According to the common notion,
they were a sect; but, according to several writers,
they were a class or profession.

We may here add a few names to the list of the
philosophers who belong to the period anterior to the
sophistical school :

Diogenes of Apollonia, born in Crete, in 498, is somewhat spiritualistic. He admits a first cause, but that first cause is the soul of the universe; that soul is spread everywhere, hence all the beings have a soul. He was a disciple of Anaxagoras, and belongs to the school of the dynamical philosophers. According to him, air is the primary element. We have some fragments of his book on Nature (Περὶ φυσεῶς), which was much praised by the ancients.

Anaxagoras was a native of Clazomenæ, where he was born in 500. He admits a first cause—eternal, creative, first motor; it is the νοῦς, which differs from ψυχή, like *animus* and *anima*. He denies the evidence of the senses, as an infallible motive of certitude, hence skepticism. Anaxagoras was very learned, and he had Pericles among his pupils. We have some fragments of a book on Nature, which was of great merit. They may be seen in Simplicius, a Greek commentator of Aristotle, in the seventh century A. C.

Parmenides was born at Ælea, in 520, and was a poet and philosopher. He is altogether a materialist, making the soul itself a material substance; he admits, of course, the eternity of matter. Some fragments have come down to us, through Sextus Empiricus and Simplicius, about his poem Περὶ φυσεῶς. It is said by Suidas that he composed several prose writings, but this is surely not exact. He was a friend of Socrates, and Plato gives a dialogue which, he pretends, took place between him and Socrates.

Zeno, called the Æleatic, who, according to Seneca, reached the highest point of skepticism. We have no writing from him, but we know he was the first who wrote his arguments under the form of dialogues.

Melissus was the teacher of Themistocles, and was born at Samos, in 482. He was also a philosopher and a poet. Melissus was an idealist.

Empedocles was born at Agrigentum, about 444, and was a poet, an historian, a philosopher, and especially a surgeon. But little is known of his doctrine, or of his life and death. Generally he is considered as a pantheist. Deity is every thing; every thing is an apparent form of God. We have some fragments from him, which have been lately published at Leipsic by Sturz.

Socrates, born at Athens, in 468, was first a sculptor, and then a soldier. He studied philosophy, and gave a system which made a complete revolution in philosophy. His life was apparently very useful, and a model, as far as such a word may apply to a case which belongs to paganism. He was attacked by Aristophanes, fell into disgrace among the people, was accused of several crimes, and sentenced to death. He was seventy years old when he died.

Socrates was not a writer. His philosophy may be divided into three parts: 1. Concerning God; 2. Concerning the immortality of the soul; 3. His moral theory. Socrates admits one God—first cause, intelligent, omnipresent, omniscient, ruling every thing; the soul is a portion of God, and is immortal. He gives nothing definite about the other life; our soul being a portion of the Deity, our duty must be to render ourselves independent from sensual appetites, and, consequently to mortify ourselves and to practise virtue. Virtue, according to Socrates, is synonymous with wisdom, hence the end of our life is the cultivation of the intellect, and the acquisition of knowledge.

The doctrine is known by the writings of his disciples; it gave rise to the schools which appeared after him, and were called from the places where they had been established. We shall give them briefly, since the present sketch belongs to the history of philosophy rather than to that of ancient literature:

1. THE CYRENAIC SCHOOL.—This school was established by Aristippus, in 465. It was an Epicurean school. The principle of Aristippus was, that all things were subservient to the use and pleasure of man. Socrates had taught that happiness was the chief good, and that it should be sought for in intellectual pleasure. Aristippus also accepts, like his master, that happiness is the chief good, but that it should be sought for in sensual pleasures. Diogenes Laërtius gives a long list of books whose authorship is ascribed to Aristippus, though he also says that, according to several authors, he wrote nothing. Among these are treatises Περὶ Παιδείας, Περὶ Ἀρετῆς, Περὶ Τύχης, and many others. Some epistles attributed to him are deservedly rejected as forgeries by Bentley.

2. THE MEGARIC SCHOOL.—This school was founded by Euclid, the namesake of the great Alexandrian geometer. The character of his philosophy was mostly logic. Euclid, who was a native of Megara, had a dialectical turn of mind, and was inclined to subtle disputations; he adopted in reasoning the indirect method, that is, the *reductio ad absurdum.* Euclid was the author of six dialogues, but no one of them has come down to us. Stilpon and Menedemus were his disciples.

3. THE CYNIC SCHOOL.—The name given to this

school comes very likely from the name of the place,
Cynosarges, where it was taught. The founder of the
Cynic school was Antisthenes, a native of Athens, and
a disciple of Socrates. The philosophy taught there,
as in the Cyrenaic school, was of a mere ethical character. Antisthenes, born in poverty, taught a contempt for external goods, and, in his outward garb and
appearance, he was himself a type and an example of
his teaching; professing poverty as a duty, he carried
his contempt for luxury to such an extent that he was
reproved by Socrates himself. He could keep but one
pupil until his death. This was Diogenes, called the
Cynic, and whose life is generally known. Antisthenes
was a skeptic in metaphysics, and his principle of morality was that virtue is sufficient for happiness, and
that any thing else must be despised. We have fragments of the writings of Antisthenes; they were collected in 1842, at Zurich.

4. THE OLD ACADEMY.—This is the name given to
the school of Plato, from Academia ('Ακαδημία), a public grove or garden in the suburbs of Athens, where
Plato established his school. The Academy was divided into the Old, the Middle, and the New. The
first one accepted purely the doctrine of the master;
the Middle Academy introduced the skeptical doctrine
of uncertainty; and the New Academy brought in what
has been termed the doctrine of probabilities.

Plato was born at Athens, in 429. His name was
first Aristocles. At the age of twenty he attended the
school of Socrates during eight years, and, at the death
of that philosopher, he travelled in Egypt, Italy, Sicily,
and visited all the philosophical schools of these coun-

tries and of his own; he then came back to Athens,
taught philosophy with success, led an edifying life,
and, after having written many works, all in the form
of dialogues, except twelve letters, he died at the age
of eighty-one.

Cicero and Quintilian profess the greatest admiration for him; he has been called "The Athenian Bee;"
his diction is elegant, melodious, and sweet; his style

PLATO.

has been censured by several modern writers, but without reason. We cannot say as much for some of his
philosophical opinions, but this question belongs to the
history of philosophy.

His works which have come down to us complete
may be divided into three classes. The first of these
is devoted to the exposition and defence of the doctrine
and life of his friend and master, Socrates; they are:
"Phædrus," "Lysis," "Protagoras," "Parmenides,"
"Apology," "Crito," "Gorgias," and "Euthyphron."

The second one contains the works written when his logical and dialectic philosophy was fully matured; they are: "Theætetus," "Meno," "Euthydemus," "Cratylus," "Sophistes," "Politicus," "Philebus," "Symposium," and "Phædon." The third one is a mixture, where the political element is predominant; these are: "Critias," "Timæus," "The Republic," and "The Laws." Xenocrates, a disciple of Plato, has left no writing.

5. THE PERIPATETIC SCHOOL. — This is the school of Aristotle.

Aristotle was born at Stagira, a town in Chalcidice, in Macedonia, in 384. At a very early age he attended the school of Plato, and remained his disciple for twenty years. Then he opened a school of his own. Aristotle studied constantly, and was very sober in his life. He became the instructor of Alexander the Great, and, after having composed very extensive works upon a great variety of subjects, he died at the age of sixty-three. Cicero calls him a man of eloquence, and praises him for his universal science, readiness, and acuteness of invention and fecundity of thought. Plato called him the philosopher of truth. Having written almost exclusively logical, metaphysical, and physical works, his style is adapted to that kind of composition. It is as clear as possible for such matters. The authority of Aristotle has been always very great, even up to our own time, although the axiom *Magister dixit* had died away. We have almost all the works of Aristotle. They may be divided:

1. Into the logic department. The extant logical writings of that philosopher are comprehended as a

whole under the title "Organon" ('Οργανον). This work is composed of six separate treatises: 1. Κατηγορία, "The Categories;" 2. Περὶ Ἑρμηνείας, "Of Interpretation;" 3. and 4. Ἀναλυτικὰ πρότερα καὶ ὕστερα, "The First and Second Analytics;" 5. Τοπικά, "The Topics," and 6. Περὶ σοφιστικῶν ἐλέγχων, "Of Sophisms."

2. In metaphysics, we have the book which bears that name, divided into fourteen parts (τὰ μετὰ τὰ φυσικά).

3. In physics. The work also bears the name of "Physics," divided into ten books: 1. The cosmology or general principles of natural science; 2. Concerning the heavens (περὶ οὐράνου); 3. On production and destruction; 4. On meteorology; 5. On the universe; 6. The history of animals (περὶ ζώων ἱστορία); 7. On the parts of animals (περὶ ζώων μοριών); 8. The generation of animals; 9. The progression of animals; 10. On the soul.

4. In the ethic department, we have the "Nichomachean Ethics," "The Eudemean Ethics," and "The Great Ethics," in which are found his treatises on economics and politics.

5. In the literary department, we have his books on the arts of rhetoric and poetry.

We might add to these schools the STOIC SCHOOL, established by Zeno; the SKEPTICAL, or PYRRHONIC SCHOOL, founded by Pyrrho, a native of Ælis, in the Peloponnesus, whose disciple Timon was a celebrated poet; and the EPICUREAN SCHOOL, established by Epicurus, a native of Samos, where he was born, in 342.

Those schools constitute the main divisions of the

history of philosophy among the ancients. But the study of all their systems belongs to philosophy. We have spoken more at length about Plato and Aristotle, because by the variety, the extensiveness, and the beauty of their writings, they had to be mentioned and appreciated in a literary point of view.

With Aristotle the era of Greek classical literature may be considered as having arrived at its close; the independence of Greece had perished, and with it whatever made the brilliant genius which characterizes classical antiquity.

Several writers have distinguished themselves after the era in question by the elegance of their works, and some of them are translated in the regular course. We shall speak of them in an Appendix, which may be found at the end of this volume.

PART II.

ROMAN CLASSICAL LITERATURE.

PRELIMINARIES.

The Latin language has not the plastic property which the Greek possesses; it is a harder material, nor did it show the vitality of the Greek. The Greek language outlived the Greek nationality; but it flourished only in Greece itself, and refused to take root elsewhere. Whenever, in any part of the world, a Greek settlement decayed, and the population became extinct—although Greek art, science, literature, and philosophy, had found there a temporary home—the language perished also.

The Latin language, on the contrary, was propagated like the dominion of Rome. It is incorrect to call the Greek a dead language, while the Latin is really dead; it flourished with Rome, and fell with it. The Latin has shown itself a language easy to be altered, and even so much changed that the old Roman, placed in contact with classical Latin, is almost entirely unintelligible.

The old Roman language was a compound of Oscan and Pelasgian, the languages of the two peoples who

first occupied Italy. The first is of German origin ;
the Oscans came from Lithuania. The second is of
Asiatic origin, as we know. The Sabellians and Um-
brians, who afterward invaded Latium, were branches
of the first family, while the Etruscans were Pelasgians.
All the words in Latin which resemble the Greek are
Pelasgian, the others are Oscan.

A few relics exist of the old Oscan language, and
these allow us to trace out the formation of the Latin.
The oldest monuments are : 1. The Eugubine Tables,
written 400 years before the foundation of Rome.
They were discovered in 1444, at the foot of the Ap-
ennines, near Eugubio. The letters B, G, D, and R,
are not used, but replaced by F, K, T, and S. 2. The
Bantine Table, discovered in 1793; it consists of a
brass plate covered with inscriptions, and, as the word
Bansæ occurs in the twenty-third line, it has been supposed to refer to the town of Bantia, which was situated not far from the spot where the tablet was found,
and it is therefore called the Bantine Table. The affinity may be traced out between most of the words
and their corresponding Latin.

In regard to the Pelasgian language: A record
written in that tongue was found near Perugia, in
1822, and it contains one hundred and thirty words.
The relation between the Latin and Greek may be
found easily, and also some Latin words which belong
entirely to the Pelasgian tongue. Many other discov-
eries were made in Etruria; some of them refer to the
kings of Rome.

Examples of the old Latin are numerous. The
most interesting of these are : 1. " The Sacred Chants,"

discovered in 1778, and containing the very words sung by the priests in the early times of Rome. The chant was that of the Fratres Arvales, a college of priests established by Romulus himself. The symbolic ensign of their office was a chaplet of ears of corn, and their function was to offer prayers, in solemn dances and processions, at the opening of spring.

2. "The Salian Hymn," of which the following fragments, preserved by Varro, are all that remain, with the exception of a few isolated words:

> "Cozolodoizesa, omina vero ad patula coemisse,
>   Jans casiones, duonus ceruses dunzianus vevet."

This has been corrected, arranged in the Saturnian metre, and translated into Latin, as follows:

> "Choroi-aulodos eso, omina enim vero
>   Ad patula ose misse Jani cariones.
>   Duonus Cerus eset, dunque Janus vevet."

"Choroio-aulodus ero, omina enim vero ad patulas aures miserunt Jani curiones. Bonus Cerus erit donec Janus vivet."

[I will be a flute-player in the chorus, for the priests of Janus have sent omens to open ears. Cerus (the Creator) will be propitious, so long as Janus shall live.]

3. "The Leges Regiæ" are generally considered as furnishing the next examples, in point of antiquity, of the old Latin language; but, there can be little doubt that, although they were assumed by the metrical traditions to belong to the period of the kings, they belong to a later historical period than the laws of the Twelve Tables. Some fragments of laws, attributed to Numa and Servius Tullius, are preserved by Festus in a restored and corrected form, and therefore it is to be

feared that they have been modernized in accordance with the orthographical rules of a later age.

4. Some fragments have been preserved by Cicero, Aulus Gellius, Ulpian, and others, of the Latin of the Twelve Tables. These laws were graven on tablets of brass, and publicly set up in the Comitium, and were first made public in 449 B. C.

5. The Tiburtine inscription, which was found in the sixteenth century, at Tivoli, comes next. It was in the possession of the Barberini family, but it was afterward lost, and has never been recovered. It was a "Senatus Consult.," written during the second Samnite War. The Latin in which it is written may be considered almost classical, the variations from that of a later age being principally orthographical.   For example:

Tiburtes	is written	Teiburtes.
Castoris	"	Kastorus.
Advertit	"	Advortit.
Dixistis	"	Deixsistis.
Publicæ	"	Poplicæ.
Utile	"	Oitile.
Inducimus	"	Indoucimus.
A, or *ab*, before *v*,	"	Af.

6. Several epitaphs exist which were written during the Carthaginian War, and we may see by degrees the formation of the classical Latin. The following differences only are found:

In modern Latin.		In ancient Latin.
E was represented by *i*, sometimes *u;* condumnari.		
I " by *u, ei, e, o;* { optume, nominus, preivatus, dedet.		

In modern Latin.		In ancient Latin.

U was represented by *oi, ou, o ;* $\left\{ \begin{array}{l} \text{quoius, douco,} \\ \text{houc, ploirume.} \end{array} \right.$

Æ   "   by *ai ;* aidiles.

Œ   "   by *oi ;* proilium, for prœlium.

The vowels were at times doubled, as leegi, luuci, haace.

We may divide this part into three books. The first era gives the rise and progress of Latin literature. The first five centuries of the Republic belong to that period ; but, properly speaking, Rome had no literature until the conclusion of the first Punic War.

The second era ends with the death of Augustus. It comprehends the age of which Cicero is the representative, and is commonly called the "golden age of Latin poetry."

The third era terminates with the death of Hadrian. Many excellences distinguished that era; but, evidently, its decline had commenced. As the age of Augustus was distinguished by the epithet "golden," so the succeeding period was designated as the "silver" age.

BOOK I.

THE FIRST ERA.

CHAPTER I.

FIRST ESSAYS IN PROSE AND POETRY BEFORE LIVIUS ANDRONICUS.

CICERO says that in ancient times bards were accustomed to sing at the banquets. It has been with the Romans as with all other people: they had oral poetical compositions before they possessed any written literature. The oldest measure used by the Latin poets was the Saturnian. According to Hermann there is no doubt that it was derived from the Etruscans, and that, long before the fountains of Greek literature were opened, the strains of the Italian bards flowed in this metre, until Ennius introduced the heroic hexameter. The grammarian Diomedes attributed the invention of it to Nævius, and seems to imply that the Roman poet derived the idea from the Greeks. Several other writers pretend also that the Saturnian verse is of Greek origin. It is true that the Saturnian is found among the verses of Archilochus, but many circumstances induce us to think, as more probable, that the use of it by the Greek poet is an accidental coincidence,

and that the old Roman bards did not copy it from
him. The Saturnian verse consists of two parts, each
containing three feet, which fall upon the ear with the
same effect as Greek trochees. The whole is preceded
by a syllable in thesis, technically called an anacrusis.
For example :

Sum | más o | pés qui | régum | régi | ás re | frégit.

The metre in its original form was perfectly independent of the rules of Greek prosody ; its only essential
requisite was the beat, or ictus, on the alternate syllable or its representative. The only law to regulate the
stress was that of the common popular pronunciation ;
in fact, stress occupied the place of quantity. Two or
three syllables, which, according to the rules of prosody, would be long by position, might be slurred over
or pronounced rapidly in the time of one, as in the
following line :

Amném Trojúgena Cánnam | fúgene té alienigenæ.

Thus it is clear that the principles which regulated it
were those of modern versification, without the niceties
and delicacies of Greek quantity.

The subjects of those songs were probably mythological tales. Most of the poets came from Etruria.
The Romans, being men of action, could not cultivate
literature, and so, with the Romans, literature was not
of spontaneous growth ; it was the result of external
influence. It is impossible to fix the period at which
they first became subject to this influence ; but it is
clear that in every thing mental and spiritual their
neighbors, the Etruscans, were their teachers. The
influence exercised by this remarkable people was not

only religious but moral; its primary object was discipline, its secondary one refinement. To this pure culture the old Roman character owed its vigor, its honesty, and its incorruptible sternness.

For centuries the Roman mind was imbued with Etruscan literature. The first written literature of Rome was not poetry, but history written in prose. According to Livy, the first records were written on rolls of cloth; they were the "Libri Lentei" (treaties between Rome and Carthage), "The Annales Maximi," "The Commentarii Consulares," and "The Tabulæ Censoriæ." All these records, however, which were anterior to the capture of Rome by the Gauls, perished in the conflagration of the city.

Each patrician house also had its private family history, and the laudatory orations, said to have been recited at the funerals of illustrious members, were carefully preserved, as adorning and illustrating their nobility; but this heraldic literature obscured instead of throwing a light upon history, for it was filled with false triumphs, imaginary consulships, and forged genealogies.

The first attempt at written poetry were the "Fescennine Songs," composed for theatrical exhibitions. These songs, which were the elements of the primitive Latin comedy, show that the Romans possessed a natural aptitude for satire. Like the comedies of Aristophanes, which served as models, they were often very obscene; and no wonder, when we consider the morals of the time. The word "fescennine" comes probably from "fascinum," which is the same word as the Greek "phallos."

The first theatrical exhibitions of the Latins, like those of the Greeks, had their origin, not in towns, but among the rural population. At first they were innocent and gay, and their mirth overflowed in boisterous but good-humored repartee; but liberty at length degenerated into license, and gave birth to malicious and libellous attacks on persons of irreproachable character. As the licentiousness of Greek comedy provoked the interference of the legislature, so the laws of the Twelve Tables forbade the personalities of the "Fescennine Songs." "The Ludi Oscii"—which title shows their original element—gave to the comedy a character less lewd and satirical, but made it more farcical, rougher, and clownish. Such was the state of Roman literature until the middle of the third century before Christ; from that time the drama took a more distinguished character.

CHAPTER II.

DRAMATIC STYLE IN THE FIRST ERA.

The dramas written at that period were an imitation of the Greek, even as regards style; but it would have been impossible at the time of Livius to make the lyrical portions of the drama occupy such a large portion in the Latin drama as it did in the Greek.

The following writers were the authors, not only of tragedies, but also of comedies. We have from them but fragments. From the first one even we have only the titles of his tragedies, and a few verses. They must be praised, especially for the vast improvement which the Latin tongue acquired by them :

Livius Andronicus, born in 240, was a Greek from the colony of Tarentum, and, as it was the custom at that time, he became the tutor of the son of some noble Roman, who gave him his liberty. Livius translated " The Odyssey ; " but, feeling that he had a sort of vocation for writing dramas, he turned his attention to that pursuit, and became very popular. He elevated the drama above the regions of ribaldry and folly ; still the Romans did not entirely abandon their ancient representations, where buffoonery was prevalent. As we have said, we have the titles, and a few of the verses, only, of Livius's tragedies. They were all Greek subjects, and almost all translations. According to Cicero, the style was very crude ; still Livius was much read at Rome, even during the Augustan period, and Horace complained bitterly of this. Notwithstanding adverse criticisms, Livius deserves praises for the improvement introduced in the theatrical exhibitions, and in the Latin language.

The representations of Livius were made sometimes with great display. No expense was spared in putting them upon the stage ; and so, according to what Cicero says in a letter to M. Marius, when they exhibited " The Trojan Horse " and " Clytemnestra," a procession of six hundred mules, probably richly caparisoned, was introduced in the latter, and cavalry and infantry, clad in various armor, mingled in mimic combat on the scene, while three thousand bucklers, the spoils of foreign nations, were exhibited in the former.

Cneius Nævius, born in 235, was probably a Roman

by birth, but he was surely a Roman by character and affection. He wrote an epic poem on the first Punic War; but, owing to the popularity of dramatic literature, his earliest productions were tragedies and comedies, and the titles which we have, show that they were mere Greek legends or stories. Still Nævius was not a simple imitator, for he had a style of his own, and was original. He wrote several satires, and offended personages of high rank, and, on that account, he was exiled to Utica, where he died. The following epitaph was written by himself:

> "Mortales immortales flere si foret fas,
> Flerent Divinæ Camenæ Næviam poetam.
> Itaque postquam est Orcino traditus thesauro
> Obliti sunt Romani loquier Latina lingua."

Nævius has been praised by all the writers of the Augustan era. Besides his tragedies, he wrote comedies and satires, but the few fragments which remain do not allow us to judge him. We must abide by the opinion of the ancients. Ennius and Virgil discovered in him such a freshness and power that they unscrupulously copied and imitated him, and transferred his thoughts to their own poems, as they did those of Homer. We know by Horace that, in his time, Nævius's poems were universally read, and were in the hands and hearts of everybody. Cicero praises him, although he has no taste for the old national literature. Virgil has imitated his poem on the Punic War, in the fourth book of his "Æneid," when he relates the adventures of Æneas and Dido.

Before Nævius, the Saturnian was the only Italian measure which was extant. He, as a master of taste, introduced the iambic and trochaic metres; but he excluded absolutely the heroic hexameter, and it was long before the Romans could arrive at perfection in this metre. The fragments of Nævius extant are not numerous, and we will give only the following lines describing the panic of the Carthaginians. The picture is well drawn:

> " Sic Poinei contremiscunt artibus universim;
> Magnei metus tumultus pectora possidet,
> Cœsum funera agitant, exsequias ititant,
> Temulentiamque tollunt festam."

Ennius was born in Calabria in 239, and was the first literary man who, on that account, was honored with the title of Roman citizen. Ennius prepared the new era of literature, and he is admired especially for his picturesqueness and "holiness"—this word means his antiquity. He was a model for his successors, and Cicero always calls him "Our Ennius," while Horace, speaking of him, says, "Father Ennius." He was an epic, dramatic, and comic writer. It seems that Ennius was distinguished in arms as well as in letters. He was protected by the elder Scipio Africanus, whom he accompanied in most of his campaigns. Horace accuses him of having been intemperate in drinking, and this gave him the *morbus articularis* (gout), of which he died, at the age of seventy. Honors, due to his character and talents, were paid to him after his death. The following epitaph, written by himself, shows his overweening conceit, and the high estimation of his own talents, which formed a principal defect in his character:

" Adspicete, O cives, senis Enni imagini' formam.
Hic vostrum panxit maxima facta patrum.
Nemo me lacrymis decoret, nec funera fletu
Faxit.—cur? Volito vivu' per ora virûm."

To judge by the fragments of his works, Ennius greatly surpassed his predecessors, not only in poetical genius, but in the art of versification. By his time, indeed, the best models of Greek composition had begun to be studied at Rome. Ennius particularly professed to have imitated Homer; but it is, however, the Greek tragic writers whom he has chiefly imitated, and indeed it appears, from the fragments that remain, that all his plays were rather translations from the dramas of Sophocles and Euripides, on the same subjects which he had chosen, than original tragedies.

Ennius composed satires, but the fragments of these are too short and broken to allow us even to divine their subject. The great work, however, of Ennius, and of which we have still considerable remains, was his " Annals, or Metrical Chronicles," devoted to the celebration of Roman exploits, from the earliest period to the conclusion of the Istrian War. These " Annals " were partly founded on those ancient traditions and old heroic ballads mentioned by Cicero and Cato as having been sung at feasts by the guests. The work has been divided into eighteen books, by some grammarian, long after Ennius's death. In his fourteenth book, Ennius speaks of the war prosecuted by the consul Scipio against Antiochus, who was excited to wage war against the Romans by the general Hannibal. Scipio arrives at Ilium, and we find in Ennius the following apostrophe:

6

> "O patria! O divum domus Ilium, et incluta bello
> Pergama!" ....

The following lines, containing the enthusiastic exclamation of the soldiers, are equally beautiful:

> "Quai neque Dardaneeis campeis potuere perire,
> Nec quom capta capei, nec quom combusta cremari."

The poem of Ennius, called "Phagetica," is curious, as giving us much information about the luxury of the Romans in this early age. Unfortunately, we know it only from the "Apologia" of Apuleius. It was a didactic poem on edibles, particularly fish.

The most curious point connected with the literary history of Ennius is his prose translation of the celebrated work of Euhemerus, called Ἱερὰ Ἀναγραφή. The translation, as well as the original work, is lost. Some fragments, however, have been saved by St. Augustine and Lactantius. It is clear from them that there prevailed a considerable spirit of free-thinking among the Romans in the days of Ennius. The fragments of Ennius were published, in 1564, in a book called "Fragmenta Veterum Poëtarum Latinorum."

CHAPTER III.

COMEDY.

The Roman critics divided comedy into Comœdia Palliata, in which the characters and costumes were all Greek, and Comœdia Togata, and also Prætextata, in which they were Roman. The Comœdia Togàta was again divided into Trabeata, or genteel comedy, and Tabernaria, or low comedy.

Comedy, even at the time of Plautus, was as low as the Greek, for it copied the Greek models, and gave also the picture of real life at home. Our modern comic writers have imitated this form, corrected and freed from its lewdness and low standard. In almost every one of the pieces there is a sameness in the *dramatis personæ;* the principal characters are a morose and parsimonious, or a gentle and easy, father, who is sometimes also the henpecked husband of a rich wife; an affectionate and domineering wife; a young man, who is frank and good-natured, but profligate; a grasping or benevolent Hetæra, a roguish servant, a fawning favorite, a hectoring coward, an unscrupulous procuress, and a cold, calculating, slave-dealer.

The names assigned to the characters of the Roman comedy have always an appropriate meaning. Young men, for instance, are Pamphilus (dear to all), Charinus (gracious), Phœdria (joyous); old men are Simo (flat-nosed), such a physiognomy showing generally a cross-grained disposition; Chremes forms a word signifying troubled with phlegm. Slaves generally bear the names of their native country, thus: Syrus, from Phrygia; Danus, a Dacian; Byrrhia, a native of Pyrrha in Caria; Dorias, a Dorian girl; a vain-glorious soldier is Thraso, from θράσος, boldness; a parasite, Gnatho, from γνάθος, the jaw; a nurse, Sophrona, discreet; a freedman, Sosia, as having been spared in war; a young girl, Glycerium, from γλυκὺς, sweet; a judge is Crito; a courtesan, Chrysis, from χρυσὸς, gold. These examples will be sufficient to understand the practice adopted by the comic writers. It is very difficult to understand the relation which music bore to the exhibition of Roman comedy. It is clear that there was always a musical accompaniment, and that the instruments used were flutes; the lyre was only used in tragedy, because in comedy there was no chorus, or lyric portion. The flutes were at first small and simple; but, in the time of Horace, they were much larger and more powerful, as well as constructed with more numerous stops, and greater compass. It is sometimes difficult to translate the comic writers. This is owing, first, to the license which they were accustomed to use freely, and by which we may see that the language was not spoken as it was written. Besides this, many letters were dropped or slurred, hence *domnus* for *dominus*, *audin* for *audisne*, *vluptas* for *voluptas*, *en'vero* for *enim vero*, *circventus* for *circumventus*. Sometimes they added *d* to *me*, *te*, and *se*, when followed by a vowel; *reliquit med homo* for *me homo*, and also *med erga* for *me erga*. The pronunciation of English may give an idea of what the pronunciation of Latin was among the comic poets.

The above observations enable us to reduce all the metres of Terence, and nearly all of Plautus, to iambic and trochaic, especially to iambic senarii and trochaic tetrameters. Some grammarian assigns the order of merit to the authors of Roman comedy first to Statius, then to Plautus. We think that we are not obliged to accept this classification, and that Plautus comes before Statius by antiquity and by merit.

T. Maccius Plautus was born in Umbria, in 210, in the town of Sarcini. He was a contemporary of Ennius, and very young when he removed to Rome.

His name means, in the Umbrian or Oscan language, "flat feet." He turned his attention early to the stage, and made much money, which he soon lost in commercial undertakings. Then he worked for his livelihood, and composed most of his plays at that time. The following laudatory epigram, written by Varro, is found in the "Noctes Atticæ" of Aulus Gellius:

"Postquam est mortem aptus Plautus, comœdia luget,
  Scena est deserta, dein risus ludu, jocusque,
  Et numeri innumeri simul omnes collacrumarunt."

We have twenty comedies extant by him, though he composed many more. In each plot there is sufficient action, movement, and spirit; but, if we consider them in the mass, there is too great uniformity in his fables. They hinge for the most part on the love of some dissolute youth for a courtesan, his employment of a slave to defraud the father, and the final discovery that his mistress is a free-born citizen. The Latin style of Plautus excels in briskness of dialogue, as well as in purity of expression; but it has been extolled too much by some grammarians, and especially by Varro. This writer says of Plautus what he said of Plato, that, if the Muses spoke in Latin, they would borrow the language of Plautus.

We may admit that Plautus wonderfully improved and refined the Latin language, from the rude form in which he found it. The chief excellence of Plautus is generally reputed to consist in the wit and comic force of his dialogue; and the censure of Horace, reproving the ancient Romans, who admired "Plautinos sales," seems an unjust criticism. The fact is, that the Plautian comedy maintained its position on the Roman stage for at least five centuries, and was acted as late as the reign of Diocletian. The wit of Plautus often degenerated into buffoonery, but he was writing for the theatre, and not for the reader.

The following are the names of his extant comedies: 1. "Amphitryo;" 2, 3, 4. "Asinaria," "Casina," and "Mercator;" 5. "The Aulularia;" 6. "The Bacchides;" 7. "The Captivi;" 8. "The Curculio;" 9. "The Cistellaria;" 10. "The Epidicus;" 11. "The Mostellaria;" 12. "The Menæchmi;" 13. "The Miles Gloriosus;" 14. "The Pseudolus;" 15. "The Pœnulus;" 16. "The Persa;" 17. "The Rudens;" 18. "Stichus;" 19. "The Trinumus;" 20. "The Truculentus." The 2, 3, 4, depict a state of morals so revolting that it is impossible to dwell upon them. These plays are almost as lewd as those of Aristophanes, in which that writer falls into the same defect.

Molière has imitated "Amphitryon" in a piece of the same name, and which is one of the most immoral among the comedies of that French writer. His comedy "The Miser" (L'Avare) is an imitation of "The Aulularia," but surely Molière is superior to Plautus in the picture of his "Miser." Shakespeare has imitated and surpassed "The Menæchmi," or "Comedy of Errors," arising out of the exact likeness between two brothers. The plays which were the favorites of Plautus were "The Pseudolus" and "The Truculentus." In both cases the plot is simple, but the action is bustling and full of intrigue. "The Miles Gloriosus" is one of the best pieces of Plautus, and one which has been especially imitated. The prologues of Plautus deserve a special mention, and are very skilfully composed;

they introduce the comedy, and their amusing gayety puts the audience in good-humor, and secures their applause.

Cæcilius Statius.—This comic writer, who was born in Milan, and died in 586 from the foundation of Rome, flourished between Plautus and Terentius. We have forty-five titles of his comedies, but few fragments; they were all Palliatæ. The collection of the fragments, although a considerable one, is not sufficient to test the favorable opinion entertained by the critics of ancient times. Cicero speaks of his Latin as being bad; Horace, without giving his opinion completely, says, however, that Statius was superior in dignity (gravitate), and Terence in skill (arte).

P. Terentius Afer, according to some traditions, was born at Carthage, in 192. He was a slave, who taught in the house of Terentius, hence his name; his cognomen Afer indicates his origin from Africa. Terence wrote six comedies, and then left Italy and went to Greece, where he died, at the age of thirty-four years. Most of his plays are taken from the Greek stage, still he is somewhat original. The plots of Terence are judiciously laid, the incidents are selected with taste, arranged with art, and painted with exquisite beauty. He has been considered, in the delineation of characters, as surpassing all the comic poets of Rome. Terence gave to the Roman tongue its highest perfection, in point of elegance and art. He has been called by Cæsar, "Puri sermonis amator;" and Cicero says, "Quidquid come loquens, ac omnia dulcia dicens." The narrative in his plots possesses a beautiful and picturesque simplicity. In regard to what we might

call the poetical style of Terence, it has been generally allowed that he has used very great license in
his versification. The language of Plautus is more
rich and luxuriant than that of Terence, but is far
from being so uniform or so chaste. The main purpose of Plautus was to excite laughter, and consequently we find in him, as is natural, more wit, more
vivacity of action, and more variety of incidents which
inflame curiosity; but, in every other respect, Terence
is superior to him.

The following is a list of the six plays of Terence:
1. "The Andrian;" 2. "The Eunuch;" 3. "The
Heautontimorumenos;" 4. "Phormio;" 5. "Hecyra;"
and 6. "Adelphi."

It would be, perhaps, difficult to determine which
is the best of these comedies, for all are good. We
will here give the plot of the first piece, and this will
allow us to judge all the pieces of Terence:

Glycerium, a young Athenian girl, is placed under
the care of an Andrian, who educates her with his
daughter Chrysis. On his death Chrysis migrates to
Athens, taking Glycerium with her and her sister, and
is driven by distress to become a courtesan. Pamphilus, the son of Simo, falls in love with Glycerium, and
promises her marriage. Simo discovers his son's attachment in the following manner: Chrysis dies, and,
at her funeral, Glycerium approaches too near the funeral-pile; her lover rushes forward and takes her
away, when the girl bursts into a flood of tears and
throws herself into his arms. Simo had, meanwhile,
betrothed Pamphilus to Philumena, the daughter of
Chremes, and, in order to discover his son's real senti-

ments, he pretends that the marriage with Philumena shall take place at once; Davus, a slave, advises Pamphilus to offer no opposition. At this crisis, Glycerium is delivered of a child, which Davus causes to be laid at the door of Simo. Chremes, understanding all, refuses to give his daughter. The opportune arrival of Crito, an Andrian, discovers that Glycerium is Chremes's daughter, who had been intrusted to his brother Phania, now dead, when he (Chremes) left Athens. Consequently, Glycerium is married to Pamphilus, and Philumena is given to a young lover (Charinus), who had hitherto pressed his suit in vain. The talent of Terence for narrative is displayed in this piece, especially in the scene near the funeral-pile. Molière has borrowed much from Terence. The remaining comic poets will require but brief notice.

L. Afranius wrote many comedies of the lowest class —Fabulæ Tabernariæ. He was a man of low tastes and profligate morals. We have fragments, and many titles, of his compositions.

Cicero quotes several times the name of **Atilius**— whom he calls Poëta Durissimus—and he gives one line from one of his comedies.

P. Licinius Tegula left few fragments.

Lavinius Luscius, another comic writer, is severely criticised by Terence, but we have nothing from him.

Q. Trabea is quoted several times by Cicero, and it is all that remains of his writings.

S. Turpilius is the last writer, from whom we have a few fragments, and the titles of some of his plays.

CHAPTER IV.

SATIRIC DRAMA—SATIRE.

TRAGEDY could never prevail in Rome until the whole Roman population had almost been changed by the gradual accession of slaves and prisoners, brought there from every place, but especially from the East. The Roman character could not appreciate tragic composition, and the people were not cultivated enough nor peaceful enough. Besides, we have seen that the tragedy was for the Greeks a real religious performance, and that it never had that character in Rome. The Romans could never have seen in those plays any thing but a secular amusement, to which they always preferred bloody games and gorgeous displays on the stage—any thing which could satisfy their characteristic ambition, and their thirst for blood. We have in this first period only five writers of tragedies. We have spoken already of Livius Andronicus, Nævius, and Ennius, whose poetical character was more didactic than tragic. The two others are Pacuvius and Attius. These five writers copied Greek models, for we have no tragedy extant of the kind—Fabulæ Prætextatæ. Seven titles only may be given for all the Latin tragic writers.

M. Pacuvius was born at Brundisium, in 220, and was a nephew of Ennius. Very little is known of his life, but he died at Tarentum, at the age of ninety years. We have from him the titles of twenty tragedies, of which few fragments remain. We may judge him by the sayings of Cicero, Horace, and Quintilian. Cicero says: "Omnes apud hunc ornati elaboratique sunt versus." Horace and Quintilian praise especially his learning. Quintilian, comparing him with Attius, says: "Virium Attio plus tribuitur, Pacuvium videri doctiorem, qui esse docti affectant, volunt;" and Horace, when speaking of the public opinion entertained concerning Attius, says:

> "Ambigitur quoties uter utro sit prior, aufert
> Pacuvius docti famam senis, Attius alti."

Among his tragedies the best was, according to these critics, "Iliona," whose first husband was Polydorus. From that piece Shakespeare took his play of "Hamlet." From no one play of Pacuvius are there more than fifty lines preserved, and these very much detached. It does not appear that his tragedies had much success or popularity in his own age.

L. Attius was born about 170. According to Cicero, his style was harsh, but he was held in great estimation by his countrymen for the force and eloquence of his productions. We have seen the opinion of Horace and Quintilian about him. Attius wrote at least fifty tragedies; none remain entire, but we have many fragments.

The following lines from "The Phenissæ" and "The Complaint of Philoctete," are, though brief, fair examples of his language and versification:

> "Sol, qui micantem candido curru atque equis
> Flammam citatis fervido ardore explicas,
> Quianam tam adverso augurio et inimico omine
> Thebis radiatum lumen ostendis tuum!"

"Heu! quis salsis fluctibus mandet
Me ex sublimi vertice saxi,
Jamjam absumor; conficit animam
Vis volneris, ulceris aestus."

These quotations are found in the "Tusculanes." The titles of some of the tragedies of Attius show that he treated some subjects entirely Roman—like "Brutus," "Decius," and "Marcellus." Varro has preserved from him the "Soliloquy of Hercules," in his "Trachiniæ," an imitation of Sophocles, forty-five lines. It is probably the best piece of Attius.

In the genus Satire—which is really a Roman invention, and the result of their passion for comedy—we have but one writer before Horace.

C. Lucilius was a Roman knight, born in 149, at Suena. In his youth he was a soldier, and, during all his life he enjoyed the greatest intimacy with the best military men of his time. Unfortunately, his writings are so mutilated that few particulars of his life and manners can be gleaned from them. He wrote thirty books of satires, and from the fragments which are extant we may judge the poet.

The time when he lived was very good for a satiric writer, for it was the time of transition between the austere way of living of the Romans, and the introduction of foreign luxury and exaggerated refinement. The chief characteristic of Lucilius was his vehement and cutting satire. He is called by Macrobius, "Acer et violentus poëta." His Latin, according to Horace, was sufficiently pure, but his versification was rugged and prosaic. Horace compares his poetry to a muddy and troubled stream; but, from the opinion of Quintilian, we may judge that this is exaggerated. For Quintilian, while blaming those who considered Lucilius as the greatest of poets, does not coincide with the opinion of Horace when he says: "Ego quantum ab illis, tantum ab Horatio dissentio, qui Lucilium fluere lutulentum, et esse aliquid quod tollere possis, putat."

Lucilius, it is true, has occasionally used too much license, as, when he barbarously separated the syllables of a work, like in the following line:

"Villa *Lucani*—mox potieris *aco*."

The satires of Lucilius must have possessed nobler qualities than those of style. The poet was a man of high moral principle, and devotedly attached to the cause of virtue, a relentless enemy of vice, and a gallant and fearless defender of truth and honesty. Like Juvenal, he felt "difficile est non satiram scribere." No wonder, then, that we find him eloquent when he speaks of virtue, as in the following passage preserved by Lactantius:

"Virtus, Albine, est pretium persolvere verum
  Queis in versamur, queis vivimu' rebu' potesse,
  Virtus est homini scire id quod quæque habeat res.
  Virtus, scire homini rectum, utile, quid sit honestum,
  Quæ bona, quæ mala, item quid inutile turpe inhonestum.
  Virtus, quærendæ finem rei scire modumque;
  Virtus, devitiis pretium persolvere posse.
  Virtus, id dare quod reipsa debetur honori,
  Hostem esse atque inimicum hominum morumque malorum;
  Contra, defensorem hominum morumque bonorum;
  Magnificare hos, his bene velle, his vivere amicum;
  Commoda præterea patriai prima putare,
  Deinde parentum, tertia jam postremaque nostra."

CHAPTER V.

PROSE—HISTORY.

WE have many fragments extant from the writers of history belonging to this first era. We might say that all their writings have been preserved in the compositions of the historians of the following centuries. Since we have no complete work from any of them, we will but give the names, and add a few brief remarks upon each of them.

Q. Fabius Pictor, who lived in the time of Nævius, was the first Roman who wrote an historical account of his country. Livy called him "scriptorum antiquissimus." We have but few fragments of his writings, and quotations in Dionysius Halicarnassus, Plutarch, and Livy. Evidently he accepted as truths the many fabulous events, and, no wonder, since he had but the obscure traditions of those primitive ages. Livy copied him too much. The name of Pictor was given to his grandfather, who was a celebrated painter, and who decorated the Temple of Salus, dedicated 302 B. C. That temple could be seen in the time of Claudius, when it was burned. The book of Fabius was written in Greek; its loss is not to be regretted.

L. Cincius Alimentus was a contemporary of Fabius. He is quoted by Livy, and Aulus Gellius, as having written in Greek a history of Rome, and a treatise, "De Re Militaria." The two books are lost.

Acilius Glabrio was born in 210 B. C. He also wrote a history in Greek, which was translated into Latin by Claudius, and referred to often by Livy. The book is lost.

M. Porcius Cato Censorinus.—This great man was born at Tusculum, in 232, of an humble family; he was the grandfather of M. Cato Uticensis. After many years spent on a farm, where he led a perfect life, in the pagan acceptation of that word, he was induced to go to Rome, where he commenced his public career. Cato, as a military man, as an administrator, and as a counsellor, had a career very useful and very brilliant. We might enter here into many particulars referring to his life, but we have to consider Cato in this sketch as a literary man only. His name of Censorinus arises from his zeal for the keeping of the laws at Rome, and from his efforts in order to prevent the Romans from departing from their ancient customs. He wrote many books, but we have only one extant, and very likely this is not complete, since we do not find in it some references pointed out by Livy. The work we have is "De Re Rustica," a mere treatise on husbandry, written without order, in one hundred and sixty-two chapters, for his son. The style is familiar, and, among many other things, we find in it the notions of the most virtuous Roman about slaves. When they are old and sick, Cato classes them: "Ferramenta vetera, servum senem, servum morbosum, et si quid aliud supersit vendat."

Cato wrote one hundred and fifty orations, which were extant in the time of Cicero, and were much praised by him. He wrote a book on military discipline, but the one whose loss is most to be deplored is his work, in six books, "De Originibus." It was a history of the kings of Rome, often quoted by Cornelius Nepos, who has given us the substance of it. He also wrote a book on medicine, the fruit of his experience. His "Apophthegmata" are spoken of by Cicero, in his book "De Officiis." He also wrote a "Carmen de Moribus," which carmen, it seems, was not written in verse. A book, containing the "Origines" of Cato, was published in 1498, under the title "Antiquitates Variæ," but it contained only spurious fragments. We may judge of the appearance of Cato by the following epigram:

Πυρρὸν, πανδακέτην, γλαυκόμματον, οὐδὲ θανόντα
Πόρκιον εἰς ἀΐδην Περσεφόνη δέχεται.

Which we may translate: "With his red hair, constant snarl, and gray eyes, Proserpine would not receive Porcius, even after death, into Hades." Of the orations of Cato ninety titles are extant, and numerous fragments. His style was abrupt, concise, witty, and full of contrast.

After Cato we have many historians of whose works fragments only are extant. We may give the names of **Hemina**, who wrote five or six books of Roman annals, in which many fables were found. After him, **Fabius Maximus Servilianus** (150), **Fannius**, and **Vennonius**, wrote annals, the fragments of which show that their Latin was not very elegant.

P. Sempronius Asellio wrote a memoir on the Numantian War.

C. Julius Gracchanus wrote a constitutional history of Rome. The work is lost, but it is often quoted by the jurists as a reliable authority.

S. **Fabius Pictor,** and **Calpurnius Piso Censorius,** also wrote annals, but Livy called Piso a liar. Piso was an honest man, but not an honest historian. Cicero speaks of him in his discourse " Pro Archia Poëta," where he also gives the names of **Æmilius Scaurus,** and **Rutilius Rufus.** Rutilius wrote autobiographies, and his example was followed by **Sulla,** who gave his memoirs in twenty-two books. All these historians, from whom we have but quotations, are praised by Cicero for their latinity.

The last historians before the second era were **Macer, C. Quadrigarius,** and **Valerius Antias.** They collected traditions, and wrote valuable books, whence Livy has taken many documents. These three writers are not praised for their style; that of Quadrigarius especially is abrupt and sententious. No Roman historian ever made greater pretensions to accuracy than Antias, and no one was less trustworthy. Livy never hesitates to call him a liar, and he is right, for he has been guilty of many falsehoods.

Two more important names remain to be mentioned among the annalists. They were **Cornelius Sisenna,** often quoted by Sallust, and **Ælius Tubero,** quoted once by Dionysius and twice by Livy.

CHAPTER VI.

PROSE—ELOQUENCE—GRAMMARIANS.

ELOQUENCE must have been an early characteristic of the Roman people—it is a plant indigenous to a free soil. There was political eloquence in a city where there was a constant struggle between the various classes of the people. There was in the army a military eloquence, to excite the heroism of the soldiers. Cicero speaks of a discourse, composed before Nævius had written any poetry; it was the discourse of Appius Claudius against Pyrrhus. Cicero had read it. Some funeral orations also, of these early times, existed in the time of Cicero. The one of Metellus, at the commencement of the second Punic War, is quoted by Livy, fourth book. Livy has preserved also the oration of Scipio Africanus Major, defending himself before the senate after the defeat of Hannibal. We have spoken of Cato, who was a real orator; the father of the Gracchi was also very distinguished. Scipio Africanus, Minor, the son of Paulus Æmilianus, and his friend Lælius, were two great orators. We have some fragments of their discourses.

The period of the Gracchi (150) produced many orators. These were Papirius Carbo, Æmilius Scaurus, Rutilius Rufus, and the Gracchi themselves; also their mother, who was the daughter of Scipio. Cicero speaks of her letters, which were extant in his time, as being models of eloquence. Several fragments only remain of all the writings of these orators.

Between the Gracchi and Cicero we had:

M. Antonius Crassus, who fell a victim to political fury. Cicero has quoted some of his most admired passages.

L. Licinius Crassus, born at Rome, in 140, was first a lawyer, but he became a political orator. His masterpiece is his oration "Pro lege Servilia," in order to return to the senate the judicial office which had been taken from it by the "Lege Semproniana." He was what may be called the most ornamental speaker that had hitherto appeared in the Forum. Though not without force, gravity, and dignity, these were happily blended with the most insinuating politeness, urbanity, ease, and gayety. He was master of the most pure and accurate language, and of perfect elegance of expression, without any affectation or unpleasant appearance of previous study. Great clearness of language distinguished all his harangues, and, while descanting on topics of law or equity, he possessed an inexhaustible fund of argument and illustration. Some persons considered Crassus as only equal to Antonius; others preferred him, as the more perfect and accomplished orator. As a public speaker, Crassus was remarkable for his diffidence in the opening of a speech—a diffidence which never forsook him—and, after the practice of a long life at the bar, he was frequently so much agitated in the exordium of a discourse as to grow pale, and tremble in every joint of his frame.

Cicero selected him to be the representative of his sentiments in the "Oratore." He felt that their tastes were congenial. Crassus almost died on the floor of the senate-house; he took the defence of the aristocratic party, and his opponent was Philippus, the consul. The controversy grew very warm, and Crassus fell in a paroxysm. This was too much for him; fever ensued, and in seven days he was a corpse.

He had the school for rhetoricians shut up because he found that it was introducing, with Greek manners, Greek corruption; but he has been blamed for that measure. We have two orations only from him.

Q. Hortensius was born at Rome, of a plebeian family, in 114. He was for some time the prince of orators, until the star of Cicero arose. They first came in contact in the cause of Quintius, and, later, in that of Verres; of course, Hortensius was beaten. But the two orators were afterward very good friends, having identical views in politics. Hortensius had a daughter who wrote discourses, and one of them was read in the time of Quintilian for the sake of its own merits.

The diction of Hortensius was noble, eloquent, and rich; his voice strong and pleasing, and his gestures carefully studied. The eloquence of Hortensius would seem, in fact, to have been of that showy species called Asiatic, which flourished in the Greek colonies of Asia Minor. This glowing style of rhetoric, though deficient in solidity and weight, was not unsuitable in a young man, being further recommended by a beautiful cadence of periods, and attended by the utmost applause. But Hortensius, as he advanced in age, did not correct this exuberance, nor adopt a chaster eloquence; and this luxury and glitter of phraseology, which, even in his earliest years, had occasionally excited ridicule and disgust among the graver fathers of the senatorial order, being totally inconsistent with his advanced age and consular dignity, which required something more serious and composed, his reputation, in consequence, diminished with the increase of years.

Hortensius, who was most extravagant in his life, owes perhaps to the friendship of Cicero the acquisition of some celebrity, for he was very vain, and remained a young man all his life. There was only one oration extant from him in the time of Quintilian.

Toward the conclusion of this literary period a great increase took place in the numbers of those learned men whom the Romans termed "literati," but who afterward were called, according to the Greek custom, "grammatici" (grammarians). Few of them were authors, but, owing to their learning, they exercised a powerful influence over the public mind as professors, critics, and school-masters. We may mention the names of **Lenæus,** a freedman of Pompey the Great ; of **Servius Clodius,** a Roman knight; and also of **Ælius Stilo,** and **Valerius Cato,** who was a poet.

We have traced the rise and progress of Roman literature ; the dawn has gently broken, the light has steadily increased, and is succeeded by the noonday brilliance of the Golden Age.

BOOK II.

DURING this period Roman literature attained the highest point of perfection; this time was above 680 years from the foundation of Rome, when Cicero was between thirty and forty years old. Poetry still continues to improve during this period, for we find much difference between the verses of Lucretius and those of Virgil, in regard to metrical structure and diction. The dramatic literature disappeared, and was replaced by the Mimes, a sort of entertainment which acquired much popularity. There was a great difference between the Greek mimes and the Latin ones. The Greek mimes were without verse; they were dialogues, not dramatic pieces, and were never exhibited on the stage. The Roman mimes were laughable imitations of manners and persons, and so combined features of comedy and farce. It was a pantomime, where mimicry and burlesque dialogue were accidentally introduced. After a time the dialogue occupied a more prominent position, and was written in verse. We have, during the Golden Age, two writers of mimes who acquired much celebrity.

CHAPTER I.

POETRY.

Section I.— Writers of Mimes.

Decius Laberius.—He was a Roman knight, but, although the profession of an artist was infamous for a man of his rank, he could not resist the temptation, and became an actor and an author. He wrote forty-three mimes; we have but the titles and a few fragments of them. We may judge by them of the qualities of Laberius; he was very sarcastic, very witty, very prompt and happy in his answers. He showed also much boldness in several circumstances. His style was very good.

In order to judge of his quickness and readiness in repartee, we have but to quote the following verses. While, one day, he had been vanquished by his adversary Syrus, Cæsar said to him with a sneer:

"Favente tibi me, victus es, Liberi, a Syro."

He replied with the following sad but true reflections:

"Non possunt primi esse omnes omni in tempore,
Summum ad gradum cum claritatis veneris
Consistes ægre; et quum descendas decides;
Cecidi ego, cadet qui sequitur, laus est publica."

C. Matius was called Calvena on account of his baldness. His mimes were called Mimiambi, because he wrote in the iambic measure. He was especially remarkable for his skill in the introduction of new words.   We can judge him only by the quotations of Cicero, as none of his pieces are extant.

Publius Syrus was a slave from Syria, and was freed by Publius, hence his double name; he wrote many mimes, but we have none left.   What remains from Syrus are eight or nine hundred maxims, very seldom exceeding one line, but containing reflections of un-rivalled force, truth, and beauty, on all the various re-lations, situations, and feelings of human life.   Those maxims were a sort of store of commonplaces and pre-cepts of morality, which they could introduce appro-priately in their extemporaneous performances.

The mimes, soon after Augustus, were replaced by Pantomimes, exhibitions which threw a great discredit on the stage, on account of their being sensual and licentious.   Even under the reign of Augustus, the pantomime was already popular.

Section II.—Elegiac Poetry.

C. Valerius Catullus was born at Verona, in 86.   He came very early to Rome, where he led a profligate life, and died when he was but thirty years old; some, however, say when he was forty-one years of age.   His poems, which are numerous, are chiefly employed in the indulgence and consummation of his loves.   They have been divided in lyric, elegiac, and epigrammatic. He seems to have been the earliest lyric poet of Latium, although Horace claims the same honor.   Much of his poetry appears to have been lost.

Many of his amatory trifles are quite unrivalled in the elegance of their playfulness, and no author has excelled him in the purity and neatness of his style, the delightful ease and simplicity of his manner, and his graceful turn of thought and happiness of expression. Some of his productions breathe the highest enthusiasm of the art, and are colored with a singular picturesqueness of imagery. Catullus was well versed in Greek literature, and he translated many of the shorter and more delicate pieces of the Greeks. Here is an example; it is a translation of an elegy of Sappho:

> "Ille mî par esse Deo videtur,
> Ille, si fas est, superare divos,
> Qui sedens adversus, identidem te
>   Spectat et audit.

> "Dulce ridentem: misero quod omnis
> Eripit sensus mihi; nam simul te,
> Lesbia, aspexi, nihil est super mî
>   Voce loquendum.

> "Lingua sed torpet; tenues sub artus
> Flamma dimanat; sonitu suopte
> Tinniunt aures; gemina teguntur
>   Lumina nocte."

In all his verses, whether elegiac or heroic, we perceive his imitation of the Greeks. His Hellenisms are frequent, and his images, similes, metaphors, are all Greek. We have seen a translation; let us give a specimen of his own composition in the elegiac style. He wrote it after having visited the grave of his brother, buried in Asia:

> "Multas per gentes, et multa per æquora vectus,
> Adveni has miseras, frater, ad inferias.
> Ut te postremo donarem munere mortis
> Et mutum nequidquam alloquerer cinerem.

7

> Quandoquidem fortuna mihi tete abstulit ipsum
>   Has miser indigne frater adempte mihi!
> Nunc tamen interea prisco quæ more parentum
>   Tradita sub tristes munera ad inferias
> Accipe fraterno multum manantia fletu
>   Atque in perpetuum, frater, ave atque vale!"

Although the peculiar characteristics of his poetry are chiefly to be found in his lyric and elegiac poems, there are in his longer pieces, which are less known and less admired, passages of singular sweetness and beauty. Catullus had not sufficient grasp and comprehensiveness of mind to conduct an epic poem. The poem entitled "The Marriage of Peleus and Thetis," bears some resemblance to an heroic poem. The most beautiful passage is the episode relating the story of Theseus and Ariadne, commencing with the following verses:

> "Siccine discedens, neglecto numine divûm,
>   Immemor ah! devota domum perjuria portas?
> Nulla ne res potuit crudelis flectere mentis
> Consilium? tibi nulla fuit clementia præsto,
> Immite ut nostri vellet mitescere pectus?"

There were living at Rome, in the time of Catullus, several poets, who wrote elegiac verses, but whose compositions are not extant. Very likely their merits did not satisfy the fastidious taste of the Augustan age, and this is the reason why Horace and his contemporaries did not preserve their writings. They were Licinius Calvus, Helvius Cinna, Valerius Cato, Valgius, Ticida, and Varro Atacinus. All these poets are mentioned by Virgil, Pliny, Suetonius, and, in general, by the grammarians.

Albius Tibullus, born probably in 54 before Christ, was a contemporary of Virgil and Horace. He was of an equestrian family. During the trouble of the civil wars he lost his paternal estate, and owed his fortune to the favors of Mæcenas. He wrote four books of elegies; the style and tone are, like his character, deficient in vigor and manliness, but sweet, smooth, polished, tender, and never disfigured by bad taste. He does not deserve the censure of Niebuhr, who stigmatizes him as a disagreeable poet because of his doleful and weeping melancholy. The characteristics of Tibullus are simplicity, and natural and unaffected genius. His elegies celebrate the beauty, inconstancy, and cruelty of his mistresses. Tibullus died young, shortly after Virgil, if we may trust the following epitaph, contained in the "Latin Anthology:"

> "Te quoque Virgilio consitem non æqua, Tibulle,
>   Mors juvenem campos misit in Ælysios,
> Ne foret, aut elegis molles qui fleret amores,
>   Aut caneret forti regia bella pede."

Some writers pretend, and their opinion is, probably, that two only of the four books of Tibullus's elegies are genuine, and these are the third and fourth.

S. Aurelius Propertius.—Very little is known concerning the life and personal history of Propertius. He was born in Umbria, about 700 from the foundation of Rome, and, like his contemporaries—Virgil, Horace, and Tibullus—he was a sufferer from the consequences of the civil wars. Propertius cultivated poetry at a very early age but, his imitations from the Greek are too studied, and too apparent, to permit him to lay claim to great natural genius. Nature alone could give the touching tenderness of Tibullus, and the facility of Ovid. The absence of original fancy is concealed by minute attention to the outward form of poetry. His pentameters are often inharmonious.

According to Quintilian, the critics of his day somewhat overrated his merits, for they could scarcely decide the question of superiority between him and Tibullus; but, evidently, the solution is easy. Propertius is far below Tibullus for natural talent and genius. His poetry is not so polluted with indelicacy as that of Ovid, but still it is often sensual and licentious. We have four books of elegies from Propertius, and, if we except those of the fourth book, consecrated mostly to the praises of Augustus. Those found in the first three refer almost always to his mistress Cynthia, and, according to Martial, she owes to him her immortality, while he owes to his love for her the inspiration which immortalizes him:

> " Cynthia, facundi carmen juvenile Properti,
>   Accepit famam nec minus illa dedit."

The date of the poet's death is unknown, but the probability is that he died young, at the age of forty.

C. Cornelius Gallus was born in 66 before Christ, and was more distinguished as a general than as a poet. Except a single line from one of his elegies, not a vestige remains of his poetry, and the pieces attributed to him are not genuine. No judgment respecting his merits can be formed from the contradictory criticisms of the ancients.

Section III.—Epigrammatic and Didactic Poetry.

C. Cilnius Mæcenas, the first minister of Augustus, the great friend of Virgil and Horace, the protector of *savants* of that period, wrote verses; but, from the confession of all the critics, his attempts at poetry were very contemptible; still, by his good taste and munificence, he exercised a great influence upon literature, and the literary men of Rome were much indebted to him for the use which he made of his confidential friendship with Augustus. Few fragments remain of his epigrams. The following lines will show sufficiently, among many defects, his unintelligible obscurity:

> "Sole et Aurora rubent plurima
> Inter sacra movit aqua fraxinos:
> Ne exequias quidem unus inter miserrimos
> Viderem meas."

C. Valgius Rufus was a great favorite of Horace. We have no records of his life, and of his writings only a few short isolated passages are extant. We find three quotations in Quintilian; Seneca mentions him, and Pliny praises his erudition.

L. Varius Rufus was one of the constant guests of Mæcenas's table. Scarcely any thing is known of him. The titles of two of his poems are extant: 1. "De Morte;" 2. "Panegyric of Augustus." Of the former, four fragments are preserved by Macrobius; of the latter, two lines have been preserved, and are found introduced in the sixteenth epistle of the first book of Horace.

Æmilius Macer wrote a poem which is only known through two verses of the "Tristia" of Ovid, which

state that it treated of birds, serpents, and medicinal
herbs.   He was born at Verona, and died in Asia, 16
after Christ.   Here are the two verses of Ovid :

"Sæpe suus volucres legit mihi grandior ævo.
Quæque necet serpens, quæ juvet herba Macer."

Quintilian compared his poem to the one of Lucretius,
and said that Macer was superior in elegance, but that
the style was deficient in dignity.

Ovidius Naso was born at Salmo (Abruzzi), on the
day of the murder of Cicero, in the year 43 B. C.   His
family was equestrian, and had been so for some gener-
ations.   Ovid had a brother, one year elder than himself; they both went to Rome, when they were young,
and studied rhetoric under good masters.   We may
see, by the discourse of Ajax and Ulysses, that Ovid
was a good rhetorician; but he felt that he had a vocation for poetry, and, although, in order to comply
with his father's wishes, he cultivated eloquence, and
left aside poetry, still he was a poet against his own
will, for whatever he wrote was verse.

His rank, talent, and fortune, enabled him to cultivate the society of the literary men of his age, but already Horace and Virgil, and also Tibullus, had gone.
Ovid was married three times; he was twice divorced,
but loved his third wife sincerely, who belonged to the
Fabian family.   Ovid was an Epicurean in his tastes,
and a skeptic, and he lived a life of continual self-in-
dulgence and intrigue.

Ovid was popular as a poet, he was successful in
society, and he possessed all the enjoyments which
wealth can bestow.   But this sunny life at length came

to an end; when his hair became tinged with white, and he had reached his fiftieth year, he incurred by some fault the anger of Augustus, and was banished to Tomi. This place, situated at the mouth of the Danube, in the country of the Getæ, has a very unpleasant and unhealthy climate. Ovid went there in winter, and there lived ten years. He died at the age of sixty-one.

Most of the poems of Ovid might be considered as elegiac, but his "Metamorphoses," which constitute the best part of his writings, were didactic, and to that style also belongs "The Art of Love." One of his earliest works are his "Amores," a collection of elegies, most of which are addressed to his favorite Corinna. They form three books. Licentiousness disfigures these annals of his "Amours;" some passages even are so lewd that they have never been translated. This work shows a wonderful talent for poetry. The twenty-one "Epistolæ Heroidum" (epistles to and from women of the heroic age) are a series of love-letters; their characteristic feature is passion. Their great merit consists in the neatness of the sentiments expressed, and the sweetness of the versification; their great defect is the want of variety.

"The Art of Love" shows the grossness into which love had fallen at the time of Ovid; it had nothing chivalrous and pure, but it was carnal and sensual. The instructions contained in the first two books, addressed to men, are fit only for the seducer. The third is fit only for abandoned women. "The Remedies of Love" followed "The Art of Love." "Let him," says Ovid, "who taught you to love, teach you also to cure;

one hand shall inflict the wound and minister the balm." His "Metamorphoses" consist of fifteen books, and contain a series of mythological narratives from the earliest times to the translation of the soul of Julius Cæsar to heaven, and his metamorphosis into a star.

This poem is Ovid's noblest effort; it approaches very near to the epic form. We admire everywhere his natural facility in versification, his picturesque truthfulness and force, the richest fancy combined with grandeur and dignity. Among the most beautiful portions may be enumerated the "Story of Phaeton" in which the description of the palace of the sun is especially remarkable; "The Golden Age," "Philemon and Baucis," "The Adventures of Pyramus and Thisbe," "Narcissus at the Fountain," "The Cave of Sleep," "Dædalus and Icarus," "The Soliloquy of Medea." A more extensive knowledge of mythology may be derived from this book than from the Greeks themselves. It is good to notice that the twelve concluding books were not reviewed by the author; Ovid left for Tomi, not having had time to correct his poem, and he had no opportunity afterward to attend to that correction. He therefore thought it necessary to apprise his friends in Italy that the work had not received his last emendations, and, as an apology for its imperfections, he proposes that the six following lines should be prefixed as a motto to the copies of his "Metamorphoses" which were then circulating in the capital ("Tristia" i., 6):

> "Orba parente suo quicumque volumina tangis;
> His saltem vestra detur in urbe locus.

Quoque magis faveas, non hæc sunt edita ab ipso,
  Sed quasi de domini funere rapta sui.
Quicquid in his igitur vitii rude carmen habebit,
  Emendaturus, si licuisset, erat."

"The Fasti" is an antiquarian poem of the Roman calendar. Ovid completed only the first six books; he intended to have twelve, one for each month.

"Sex ego Fastorum scripsi, totidem que libellos
  Cumque suo finem mense volumen habet."

It is a beautiful specimen of simple narrative in verse, and it displays better than any of Ovid's writings his power of telling a story in poetry as well as in prose.

The five books of the "Tristia," and the four books of "Epistles from Pontus," were the outpourings of his sorrowful heart during the gloomy evening of his days. There is not so much wit and genius as in his former compositions, but they are conceived in the spirit of the Greek elegy. His minor poems consist of an elegiac poem, "Nux," in which he gives the fate of a nut-tree; a satire, "Ibis," which is a very bitter composition, most likely against some faithless friend; a poem entitled "Medicamina Faciei," on cosmetics; another on fishing ("Halientica"), referred to often by Pliny in his "Natural History," and an address of condolence to Livia Augusta. Ovid was also the author of a tragedy called "Medæa," which has been analyzed and praised by Quintilian, but of which only two verses are extant. To recapitulate, Ovid was a very good elegiac and didactic poet. Four poets lived at the time of Ovid. They were:

Gratius Faliscus, Pedo Albinovanus, A. Sabinus, and M. Manilius. The first left a poem, in five hundred and thirty-six lines, called "Cynegetica," treating of the chase, hares, and hounds. The style is harsh and prosaic. Of the next two no writings are extant, and the last one (Manilius) wrote an astronomical and astrological poem, in which he gives the doctrine of a stoical pantheism. It is an incomplete and poor work.

Section IV.—Epic Poetry.

Lucretius Carus was born in the year 95 B. C. Little is known of his life. According to Eusebius he died at the age of forty-four years, by his own hand, in a

LUCRETIUS.

paroxysm of insanity produced by a philter, which Lucretia, his wife or mistress, had given him, with no design of depriving him of life or reason, but to renew or increase his passion.

He wrote a poem, in six books, "De Rerum Natura," which we have. It is philosophic and didactic, and contains a full exposition of the theological, physical, and moral system of Epicurus. Notwithstanding the nature of the subject, which gave the poet little opportunity for those descriptions of the passions and feelings which generally form the chief charm in poetry, Lucretius has succeeded in imparting to his work much of the real spirit of poetry, and, no doubt, if he had chosen a subject which would have afforded him greater scope for the exercise of his powers, he might have been ranked among the first of poets. In no writer does the Latin language display its majestic and stately grandeur so much as in Lucretius. There is a power and an energy which we rarely meet with in the Latin poets; and no one who has read his invocation to Venus, at the beginning of the poem, or his delineation of the demons of superstition, and of the sacrifice of Iphigenia, which we give in part below, or his beautiful picture of the busy pursuits of men at the commencement of the second book, or the progress of the arts and sciences in the fifth, or his description of the plague which desolated Athens, during the Peloponnesian War, at the close of the sixth, can refuse to allow Lucretius a high rank among the poets—in the epic style—of antiquity.

In the whole history of Roman taste and criticism, nothing appears so extraordinary as the slight mention that is made of Lucretius by succeeding Latin authors. This, however, might be caused by the materialism of his philosophy. The works of Lucretius, like one of Virgil's, had not received the finishing touches of its author at the period of his death. We add the passage alluded to before, and we will notice how beautifully the poet has caught the spirit and feeling of Greek fancy, and how capable the Latin language now was of adequately expressing them :

> "Aulide quo pacto Triviai virginis aram
> Iphianassai turparunt sanguine fede
> Ductores Danaum delectei, prima virorum
> Cui simul infula, virgineos circumdate comtus,
> Ex utraque pari malarum parte profusa est ;
> Et mæstum simul ante aras astare parentem.
> Sensit, et hunc propter ferrum celare ministros,
> Aspectuque suo lacrumas effundere civeis ;
> Muta metu, terram genibus submissa, petebat ;
> Nec miseræ prodesse in tali tempore quibat,
> Quod patrio princeps donarat nomine regem.
> Nam sublata virum manibus, tremebunda que, ad aras
> Deducta est ; non est, solemni more sacrorum
> Perfecto, posset claro comitari hymenæo ;
> Sed, casta incerte, nubendi tempore in ipso,
> Hostia consideret mactatu mæsta parentis,
> Exitus ut classi felix faustusque daretur.
> Tantum religio potuit suadere malorum."

Ovid, speaking of Lucretius, says that "his sublime strains shall never perish, until the day when the world shall be given up to destruction."

P. Virgilius Maro was born at Andes, a few miles from Mantua, in the year 70 B. C. His father was a man of low birth, who gradually acquired means to buy a farm. Virgil commenced his studies at Cremona, where he remained until he assumed the toga virilis. At the age of sixteen he retired to Milan, and afterward to Naples, where he laid the foundation of his multifarious learning.

Virgil carefully read the Greek historians, but medicine and mathematics were the sciences to which he was chiefly addicted. Very likely from Naples Virgil did not go to Rome, but went back to his native place, and twice by his talent saved his property. Being constantly in the country, and captivated by the rural beauties of "The Idyllia" of Theocritus, Virgil became ambitious of introducing this new species of poetry into his native land, and he commenced his "Bucolics."

VIRGIL.

The situation of Virgil's residence was low and humid; his delicate constitution induced him, about the year 714, when he was thirty years old, to seek for a warmer climate. Virgil first proceeded to the capital, and there his fortune rapidly increased by the liberality of Mæcenas, and he did not enjoy less favor with the emperor than with his minister. It was probably during this period of favor with the emperor and his minister that Virgil contributed the verses in celebration of the deity who presided over the gardens of Mæcenas, and wrote, though without acknowledging it, the well-known distich in honor of Augustus:

> "Nocte pluit tota, redeunt spectacula mane;
> Divisum imperium cum Jove Cæsar habet."

It seems that Bathyllus, a contemptible poet of the day, claimed these verses as his own, and was liberally rewarded. Vexed at the imposture, Virgil again wrote the verses near the palace, and under them:

> "Hos ego versiculos feci, tulit alter honores;"

with the beginning of another line—

> "Sic vos non vobis—"

four times repeated. Augustus wished the lines to be finished, Bathyllus seemed unable, and Virgil at last proved himself the author of the distich by completing the stanza in the following manner:

> "Sic vos non vobis nidificatis aves;
> Sic vos non vobis vellera fertis oves;
> Sic vos non vobis mellificatis apes
> Sic vos non vobis fertis aratra boves."

Virgil retired to Naples in 717, and he dwelt chiefly in the neighborhood of that city for the remainder of his life. He now commenced his " Georgics," by order of Mæcenas, and continued for the following seven years closely occupied with this work.

Then "The Æneid" was commenced in 724, and it occupied him until his death. Having brought "The Æneid" to conclusion, Virgil went to Greece. It was on undertaking this voyage that Horace addressed to him the affectionate ode beginning—

"Sic te Diva potens Cypri," etc.—(I., 8.)

He soon returned to Italy, and died at Brundisium, in 734; he was then fifty-one years old. His tomb lies near Naples, on the slope of the Pausilippe, with the following epitaph written by himself:

"Mantua me genuit, Calabri rapuere; tenet nunc
Parthenope. Cecini pascua, rura, duces."

In his pastoral poetry Virgil was the professed imitator of Theocritus, but Theocritus surpasses him in the variety of his portraits, and in the minuteness and accuracy of his descriptions. Still, Virgil is superior to Theocritus; his selections are very judicious and all good; he refused whatever was gross, and threw aside what was overloaded and superfluous. He made his shepherds more cultivated than even those of his own time.

"The Georgics," in four books, treat of husbandry in general; this poem is as remarkable for majesty and magnificence of diction as "The Eclogues" are for sweetness and harmony of versification. It is the most complete, elaborate, and finished poem in the Latin, and perhaps in any language. By his genius the writer has exhibited himself as a poet on topics where it was difficult to appear as such. Virgil has imitated the poem of Hesiod, especially in his first and second book, but Virgil is more natural than Hesiod.

The great merit of "The Georgics" consists in their varied digression, interesting episodes, and sublime bursts of descriptive power, which are interspersed throughout the poem. To quote any of them would be unnecessary, as Virgil and his translations are in every one's hands. It will be sufficient to enumerate some of the most striking. These are:

1. "The Origin of Agriculture," i., 125.
2. "The Storm in Harvest," i., 316.
3. "The Signs of the Weather," i., 351.
4. "The Prodigies at the Death of Julius Cæsar," i., 466.
5. "The Battle of Pharsalia," i., 489.
6. "The Panegyric on Italy," ii., 136.
7. "The Praises of a Country Life," ii., 458.
8. "The Horse and the Chariot Race," iii., 103.
9. "The Description of Winter in Scythia," iii., 349.
10. "The Murrain of Cattle," iii., 478.
11. "The Battle of the Bees," iv., 67.
12. "The Story of Aristæus," iv., 317.
13. "The Legend of Orpheus and Eurydice," iv., 453.

The subject of "The Æneid" is the settlement of the Trojans in Italy. This production belongs to a nobler class of poetry than "The Georgics," and is equally perfect in its kind. It would be absurd to suppose that Virgil intended to give instructions to princes in the art of settling colonies, or to supply Augustus with political rules for the government and legislation of a great empire. He evidently designed, not merely to deduce the descent of Augustus and the Romans from Æneas and his companions, but, by creating a perfect character in his hero, to shadow out the eminent qualities of his imperial patron; to recommend his virtues to his countrymen, who would readily apply to him the amiable portrait; and, perhaps, to suggest that he was the ruler of the world, announced of old by the prophecies and oracles of the Saturnian land. It is objected against Virgil that he has imitated. So he has; but what he has done was customary in his time—this was allowed—and Virgil has surpassed his models and is original. For instance, we find passages like the following, copied almost *verbatim* from Ennius, and which in modern times would be considered as plagiarisms, but the ancients admitted them, without reluctance :

ENNIUS. "Est locus Hesperiam quam mortales perhibebant."
VIRGIL. "Est locus Hesperiam Graii cognomine dicunt."

ENNIUS. "Qui cœlum versat stellis fulgentibus aptum."
VIRGIL. "Axem humero torquet stellis fulgentibus aptum."

ENNIUS. "Hei mihi qualis erat quantum mutatus ab illo."
VIRGIL. "Hei mihi qualis erat quantum mutatus ab illo."

But, if there be a want of originality, it is fully compensated by the variety of incidents, the consummate skill in the arrangement of them, and the interest which pervades both the plot and the incidents. Virgil has shown himself especially skilful in a species of imitation which consists in the appropriate choice of words, and the assimilation of the sound to the sense. Representing the rapid speed of horses, and the still more rapid flight of time, he says :

"Quadrupedante putrem sonitu quatit ungula campum."
—*Æneid* viii., 591.

"Sed fugit interea, fugit irreparabile tempus."
—*Georgics* iii., 284.

An unusual use of spondees represents dignity and majesty :

"Ast ego, quæ divum incedo regina!"   —*Æneid* i., 50.

A corresponding change of metre answers for an accelerated motion :

" . . . . Jamjam lapsura cadentique
Imminet assimilis . . . . "   —*Æneid* vi., 602.

The hiatus expresses the effort :

"Ter sunt conati imponere Pelio Ossam."

Many other examples might be given of that which was, in Virgil, the natural impulse of a lively fancy and a delicately-attuned ear.

Besides the compositions we have just spoken of, it is supposed, and with much probability, that Virgil has written " The Culex," " Ciris," " Moretum," " Copa," and other shorter pieces in lyric, elegiac, and iambic metres, commonly known by the name of " Catalecta." " The Culex" is a bucolic poem, relating the act of a shepherd killing a gnat that disturbed him in his sleep, and, as soon as the shepherd awoke, he saw near him a snake ready to bite him.   The shepherd, full of remorse and gratitude, raised a tomb to his benefactor, and writes the following epitaph :

"Parve culex, pecudum custos, tibi tale merenti
Funeris officium vitæ pro munere reddit."

" The Ciris" relates the legend of Scylla changed into a fish, and her father Nisus into an eagle. " The Moretum " describes the commencement of a day's employment in the field, and the preparation of a dish of *olla-podrida*, of garden herbs called *moretum*. " The Copa " represents a female waiter at a tavern, begging for custom by a tempting display of the accommoda-

tions and comforts prepared for strangers. We find in
that elegiac poem such verses and such doctrine as the
following one :

"Pereant qui crastina curant
Mors aurem vellens, Vivite, ait, venio."

All these poems are inferior to the great compositions of Virgil; but, they were written when the
poet was young.

Section V.—Didactic and Lyric Poetry.

Horatius Flaccus was born at Venusia, or Venu-
sinum, in 65 B. C. His father was a freedman, who
bought a farm near Venusia, and Horace lived there
until he was eleven or twelve years old. Then his

HORACE.

father brought him to Rome, and gave him a good
teacher. Horace studied the ancient Latin poets, and
acquired a thorough knowledge of the Greek language.
It is probable that soon after he assumed the toga vi-

rilis. He went then to Athens to pursue his studies. Athens was at that period the university of Rome, and thither the Roman youth resorted to learn language, art, science, and philosophy.

"Inter sylvas Academi quærere verum."

During the civil war under the Second Triumvirate he joined the army of Brutus, fought at Philippi, and, as he relates it himself, threw away his shield and fled. When he came back to Italy he found that his patrimony had been taken from him. He then went to Rome, and his talents soon acquired for him—with the friendship of Virgil, Mæcenas, and Augustus—the way to fortune and honors. At Rome Horace occupied a house on the pleasant and healthful heights of the Esquiline, where he resided during the winter and spring; the summer and autumn he passed at the Sabine farm, which Mæcenas had given him or procured for him. Horace, in that country place, was a great favorite with his simple neighbors, and there he found all that he ever wished for, and even more.

"Modus agri non ita magnus
Hortus ubi, et tecto vicinus jugis aquæ fons,
Et paulum sylvæ super his."   —*Satires* vi., 1, bk. 2.

Of course Horace was happy, but the death of his friends Mæcenas and Virgil grieved him very much. He himself died soon after Mæcenas, in his fifty-eighth year.

The country was the place where his heart abode, and here he displayed all the kindness of his disposition. The character of Horace is clearly developed in his writings. He acknowledged no master in philosophy, and his boast was not a vain one. He was, practically, an Epicurean. The sterling qualities of Horace were mixed with baser alloy; still, apart from some frailties excusable at that epoch, we recognize in him most of the virtues which adorn humanity outside of Faith.

The productions of Horace consist of " Odes," " Epodes," " Satires," and " Epistles." Most of the " Odes " of Horace are Greek imitations, as we may see by the following comparisons :

"Sunt quos curriculo."   —*Odes* i., 3.

$$\text{'Αελλοπόδων μέν τινας εὔφραι-}$$
$$\text{νουσιν ἵππων τιμαὶ καὶ στέφανοι·}$$
$$\text{τοὺς δ ἐν πολοχρόσοις θαλάμοις βιοτά·}$$
$$\text{τέρπεται δὲ καί τις ἐπ' οἶδμ' ἄλιον}$$
$$\text{ναί θοᾷ σῶς διαστείχων.}$$

—PINDAR, *Fragments.*

"Jam te premet mox, fabulæque Manes."

—*Odes* i., 4, 16.

$$\text{Κατθανοῖσα δὲ κεις', οὐδέποτε μναμοσύνα σέθεν}$$
$$\text{ἔσσετ' οὐδέποτ' εἰς ὕστερον, οὐ γὰρ πεδήχεις βρόδρων}$$
$$\text{τῶν ἐκ Πιερίαις. Ἀλλ' ἀφανής κέν 'Αιδα δόμοις}$$
$$\text{φοιτάσεις πεδ' ἀμαυρῶν νεκύων ἐκπεποταμένα.}$$

—SAPPHO, *Fragments.*

" Vides ut alta stet nive candidum
Soracte, nec jam sustineant onus
Sylvæ laborantes, geluque
Flumina constiterint acuto ?"   —*Odes* i., 9.

$$\text{"Τει μὲν ὁ Ζεὺς, ἐκ δ' ὀρανῶ μέγας}$$
$$\text{Χειμών πεπάγασιν δ' ὑδάτων ῥόαι.}$$

. . . . . .

Κάββαλλε τὸν χειμῶν', ἐπὶ μέν τιθεὶς
πῦρ, ἐν δέ κίρναις οἶνον ἀφειδέως
μελιχρόν· αὔταρ ἀμπι κόρσα
μαλθακὸν ἀμπιτίθει γνάφαλλον.

—ALCÆI *Fragmenta.*

"Dulce et decorum est pro patria mori.'·
—*Odes* iii., 2, 13.

Τεθνάμεναι γὰρ καλὸν ἐπὶ προμάχοισι πεσόντα
ἄνδρ' ἀγαθὸν περὶ ᾗ πατρὶδι μαρνάμενον.

—TYRTEI *Fragmenta.*

"Mors et fugacem persequitur virum."
—*Odes* iii, 2, 14.

Ὁ δ' αὖ θάνατος ἔκιχε καὶ τὸν φυγόμαχον.
—SIMONIDES.

"O navis, referunt in mare te novi
Fluctus? O quid agis? Fortiter occupa
Portum. Nonne vides, ut
Nudum remigio latus," etc. —*Odes* i., 14.

Τὸ μὲν γὰρ ἔνθεν κῦμα κυλίνδεται,
τὸ δ' ἔνθεν· ἄμμες δ' ἀν τὸ μέσσον
ναὶ φορήμεθα σὺν μελαίνα,
χειμῶνι μοχθεῦντες μεγάλῳ κάλων·
πὰρ μὲν γὰρ ἄντλος ἰστοπέδαν ἔχει,
λαῖφος δέ πᾶν ζάδηλον ἤδη,
καὶ λακίδες μεγάλαι κατ' αὐτὸ
Κάλασι δ' ἄγκυραι.

—ALCÆI *Fragmenta.*

The following quotations are mere translations:

"Nube candentes humeros amictus."
Νεφέλη εἰλυμένος ὤμους.
—HOMER, *Iliad*, ι, 186.

"Aptum equis Argos."	Ἄργεος ἱπποβότοιο. —HOMER, *Iliad*, β', 287.
"Marinæ filium Thetidis."	Παῖς ἁλίας Θέτιδος. —EURIPIDES, *Androm.*, 108.
"Mordaces sollicitudines."	Γυιοβόρους μελεδῶνας. —HESIOD, Ἔργ., 66.
"Dis miscent superis."	Ἀθανάτοις ἔμιχθεν. —PINDAR, *Isthm.*, 2, 42.
"Loquaces lymphæ."	Λαλὸν ὕδωρ.
"Fulmine caduco."	Καταιβάτης κεραυνός. —ÆSCHYLUS, *Pr. V.*, 359.
"Flagitio additis damnum."	Πρὸς αἰσχύνη κακόν. —EURIPIDES, *Rhe.*, 102.
"Obliquum meditantis ictum."	Δοχμώ τ ἀΐσσοντε. —HOMER, *Il.*, μ', 148.
"Testudinis aureæ."	Χρυσέα φόρμιγξ. —PINDAR, *Pyth.*, ά, 1.
"Nescios fari infantes."	Νήπια τέκνα. —HOMER, *Il.*, β', 311.
"Mens trepidat metu."	Δείματι πάλλει. —SOPHOCLES, *Œd. Tyr.*
"Funera densentur."	Θνῆσκον ἐπασσύτεροι. —HOMER, *Il.*, ά, 383.
"Dulce loquentem."	Ἀδὺ φωνοίσας. —SAPPHO.

We could continue to give such quotations, and show that Horace has imitated, and even almost copied passages in Pindar, Alcæus, Sappho, Homer, and the great tragical writers, especially Euripides and Sophocles. Where Horace is principally beautiful is in the

"Odes" in which he describes the pleasures of a country life, or touches on the beauties of Nature. We may give as an example the fourth ode of the third book, from the ninth verse, in which he relates an adventure which befell him in his childhood:

> "Me fabulosæ Vulture in Apulo
> Nutricis extra limen Apuliæ,
> Ludo fatigatumque somno
> Fronde nova puerum palumbes

> "Texere (mirum quod foret omnibus,
> Quicumque celsæ nidum Acherontiae,
> Saltusque Bantinos, et arvum
> Pingue tenent humilis Ferenti),

> "Ut tuto ab atris corpore viperis
> Dormirem et ursis; ut premerer sacra
> Laurosque collataque myrto
> Non sine Dis animosus infans."

"The Epodes" of Horace breathe the spirit of the satirist rather than of the lyric poet; and, surely, like his "Satires," they were written in his years of adversity. It is to be noticed that "The Epodes" were published soon after "The Satires," and, naturally, Horace could not have rid himself entirely of the bitter spirit which animated him when he wrote his satiric compositions. It would, perhaps, be better to call "The Satires" of Horace sermons; they are, in fact, desultory didactic essays, sketching boldly and good-humoredly a picture of Roman social life with its vices and follies.

"The Epistles" of Horace do not differ from "The Satires," except that in the latter composition the poet speaks, as it were, *ex cathedra*, while in "The Epistles" he discourses with the freedom with which he would converse with an intimate friend. The epistle called "Ars Poëtica, or Epistle to the Pisos," is not a treatise on poetry, but simply an outline of the history of the Greek drama, and the principles of criticism applicable to it. It is a very good composition. The versification of "The Epistles" is more smooth than that of "The Satires," but only in proportion to the superior neatness of the style generally.

To resume, the qualities in which Horace excels are his strong good sense, his clear judgment, and the purity of his taste, and it is especially in his "Odes" that his genius as a poet is displayed. They have never been equalled in beauty of sentiment, gracefulness of language, and the melody of versification. They comprehend every variety of subject suitable to the lyric muse. Not only do they evince a complete mastery over the Greek metres, but also show that Horace was thoroughly imbued with the spirit of Greek poetry, and had profoundly studied Greek literature, especially the writings of Pindar and the lyric poets.

CHAPTER II.

PROSE—ELOQUENCE.

M. Tullius Cicero was born at Arpinum, on the same day as Pompey the Great, in 106. His father belonged to a patrician family. When he was fourteen years old he went to Rome with his brother Quintus, and

8

both had very good masters, and, among them the
Greek poet Archias. When he was quite young Cicero
showed taste for poetry and wrote verses, and even obtained on that account the praises of Marius. At sixteen he took the toga, and attended the forum regu-
larly, and he studied jurisprudence. He served very

CICERO.

little in the army, but made a campaign under the
father of Pompey the Great. He then studied philosophy, and embraced the doctrine of Plato; at twenty-
five he pleaded his first cause, and in the following year
defended Roscius, who had been accused of parricide
by a favorite of Sylla. In order to strengthen his
constitution Cicero then travelled in Greece and in
Asia, and, after a few years, came back to Rome with
invigorated health, and found Hortensius at the zenith
of his glory.

He was elected quæstor and sent to Sicily at a time

when the metropolis was suffering from a great scarcity of grain; he was then thirty years old, and owed to his eloquence that rapid elevation. Cicero discharged his office nobly.

On his return home he accused Verres, and pronounced the two orations, "In Verrem de Signis" and "In Verrem de Suppliciis," showing that during his administration Verres had been cruel and dishonest, and he had him condemned. In the following year (69), that is, five years after his election as a quæstor, and when his time of office was over, he was appointed curule-ædile, and behaved himself wisely; he found that he could satisfy the people without involving himself in the extravagant expenses which were customary among his predecessors.

In 67 he obtained the prætorship, and, during that time he made his speech, "Pro Lege Manilia," in favor of Pompey, who then obtained the command of the war against Mithridates. His next ambition was the consulship, which he obtained with Antony, and he signalized himself during that time by crushing the conspiracy of Catiline, on account of which circumstance he was hailed the father of his country. Having incurred the enmity of Clodius, who accused him of having acted as a dictator in regard to the execution of the accomplices of Catiline, Cicero went into exile voluntarily, and showed in his absence that a vain man is never a man of energy.

In the year 49 he returned to Rome, and, during the struggle between Cæsar and Pompey, tried to remain neutral, but at length joined Pompey, and after the defeat of this general he was pardoned by Cæsar. At that time Cicero had domestic afflictions, and he was twice divorced. After the assassination of Cæsar he went to Greece, but came back immediately to Rome. It was the time when the struggle was going on between Octavius and Antony. For a while Antony fled, and Cicero pronounced his fourteen " Philippics " against him; but Antony came back, and formed a triumvirate with Octavius and Lepidus. Lists of proscription were formed, and Cicero was on the list of Antony. He tried to flee; but the state of the weather did not allow him to embark; he was taken, and died nobly.

Antiquity may be challenged to produce an individual so virtuous and so perfectly amiable as Cicero. But the great orator was irresolute, timid, and inconsistent; he was continually vacillating from one extreme to the other, always too confident or too dejected, and incorrigibly vain of success. The orations he is known to have composed amount to about eighty, of which fifty-nine, either entire or in part, are preserved.

Of the rhetorical works of Cicero, the most admired and finished is the dialogue "De Oratore." In the "Oratoriæ Partitiones " the subject is the art of arranging and distributing the parts of an oration, so as to adapt them in the best manner to their end.

In the dialogue "Brutus " he gives a short account of all who had ever been remarkable in Greece or Rome for eloquence, down to his own time. "The Topica " is a compendium of "The Topica" of Aristotle. The treatise "De Optimo Genere Oratorum " was originally intended as a preface to the translation of the discourse of Demosthenes, "Pro Corona." In all his works on rhetoric he accepts the principles of Aristotle, and takes his divisions. The subject is considered in three distinct lights, with reference to the case, the speaker, and the speech: 1. The case, as respects its nature, is definite or indefinite; with reference to the hearer, it is judicial, deliberative, or descriptive; as regards the opponent, the division is fourfold according as the fact, its nature, its quality, or its propriety, is called in question. 2. The art of the speaker is directed to five points; the discovery of persuasives (whether ethical, pathetical, or argumentative), arrangement, diction, memory, and delivery. 3. The speech itself consists of six parts; introduction (exordium), proposition, division, proof, refutation, and conclusion, or peroration. The oration in which Cicero illustrates this teaching, by example, is the discourse "Pro Milone."

Cicero's laudatory orations are among his happiest efforts. The best among these orations are: "Pro Lege Manilia," "Pro Marcello," "Pro Ligario," "Pro Archia," and the ninth "Philippic," which is in praise of Servius Sulpicius. But it is in judicial eloquence, especially on subjects of a lively cast, that his talents are displayed to the best advantage, as in the speeches "Pro Cælio," and "Murena," and against Cæcilius and Catiline. The character which he draws of Catiline (or "Pro Cælio") is perfect.

Among many excellences possessed by Cicero, the greatest is the suitableness of his diction to the genius of the Latin tongue. He has been accused of being too florid, too brilliant, too Asiatic, and opposed to the sublime simplicity of the Greek writers. But we must observe that the Latin language is weak comparatively, scanty and inharmonious, and requires much skill to render it expressive and graceful. Simplicity in Latin is scarcely inseparable from baldness. Latin is not a philosophical language. In that respect Demosthenes, to whom Cicero may be compared, had a great advantage over the Latin orator. The Greek language, on account of its richness, allowed Demosthenes to be more philosophical, and consequently more solid than Cicero, in his speeches; besides this consideration, the public of Athens was composed quite differently from the public assembled in the Roman Forum, in regard to knowledge and literary culture.

Cicero rather made a language than a style, yet not so much by the invention as by the combination of words. This is that "copia dicendi" which gained Cicero the high testimony of Cæsar to his inventive power. In regard to his philosophical writings, we have "De Legibus," a treatise on jurisprudence, of which three books only remain; "De Finibus Bonorum et Malorum," being a discussion of the opinion of antiquity on that question; the treatise "Academicæ Quæstiones," relates the doctrine of the Academy; the "Tusculanæ Quæstiones" is a sort of treatise on ethics; "The Paradoxa" contains the discussion of six paradoxes of the Stoics. Then we have a treatise on mythology, "De Natura Deorum." The writings "De Officiis," "De Senectute," and "De Amicitia," are three good treatises on moral duties in the different circumstances of life. The first one was written for his son. We might add to this list a sort of sketch on astronomy, "Somnium Scipionis," and a part of a treatise—"De Republica"—of which the object is very patriotic.

As a philosopher Cicero belongs to the old Academy. His merit as a philosophical writer lies in his luminous and popular exposition of the leading principles of the ancient schools. He wrote in the form of dialogues. Little remains of his historical and poetical works, and no regret can be felt for it; from the fragments which are extant, we may judge that Cicero was not a poet.

We have about one thousand "Epistles," divided into thirty-six books, sixteen of which are addressed to Atticus, three to his brother Quintus, one to Brutus, and sixteen to his different friends. These letters throw a great light on the history of the time, and give a full insight into the private character of Cicero himself, who was accustomed at all times to unbosom his thoughts most freely to his friends.

After Cicero we may give the following names:

Asinius Pollio.—He was born at Rome, in the year 76, and was a very distinguished warrior, a companion of Cæsar and Anthony, and for a time the governor of Gallia Transpadana. He was also a writer and an orator, but none of his writings remain. He had a satirical spirit, and was often unjust in his criticisms. He was the first one who established a public library, and his example was soon followed. Æmilius Paulus, Lucullus, Sulla, and Cæsar, had already private libraries, and Pollio expended the spoils of Dalmatia in founding a temple to Liberty, and furnishing it with a library. All the emperors, from Augustus down to Hadrian, established or enlarged similar institutions. Pollio died at the age of eighty.

Terentius Varro was born at Reate, a Sabine town,

situated in the Tempe of Italy, in 116 B. C. He was also a warrior, but especially a very learned man. He was the librarian of Cæsar. No Roman author wrote so much as he did, and no one read so much, except Pliny the Elder. Varro wrote five hundred books, but one only, and some fragments of another, remain. The first is "De Re Rustica," and the other, "De Lingua Latina." What is to be regretted the more is the loss of his book "Antiquitates Rerum Humanarum, et Antiquitates Rerum Divinarum." The two treatises, forming one work, were very useful to St. Augustine for the composition of his work "De Civitate Dei." Varro composed also "Satires," partly in prose and partly in verse, consisting of moral essays and dialogues. We have eighteen short epigrams, of no great merit, of his poems. Varro died at the age of eighty-nine years.

CHAPTER III.

PROSE — HISTORY.

In historical composition alone can the Romans lay claim to originality; and, in their historical literature especially, is exhibited a faithful transcript of their mind and character. We have in the Augustan age five names which are very illustrious, and we ought not to pass over without mention the names of—

L. Lucceius, the friend and correspondent of Cicero. His right to be called an historian is founded on his having commenced a history of the social and civil wars, but it was never completed and published.

L. Licinius Lucullus was the illustrious but luxurious conqueror of Mithridates. He devoted his leisure to the composition of history, and wrote in Greek a history of the Marsian War. He was a friend of Cicero, and the great orator inscribed with his name one of his books, namely, the fourth book of his "Academic Questions," in which he made Lucullus define the philosophical opinions of the old Academy.

The five great names composing the catalogue of Roman historians, during the Augustan period, are:

Cornelius Nepos, who lived in the time of Catullus, was born near Verona, and was also a friend of Cicero. Nothing particular is known about his life. All his works, which are mentioned by the ancients, are lost. They were: 1. Three books of "Chronicles," being a short abridgment of universal history; 2. Five books of "Anecdotes;" 3. "The Life of Cicero," including a collection of letters addressed to him; 4. "De Historicis," or "Memoirs of Historians." The work now extant is entitled "The Lives of Eminent Generals," in which Cornelius gives biographies of twenty generals, and short accounts of some celebrated monarchs. Although Cornelius wrote conscientiously, still Pliny accuses him of being inaccurate, and modern critics have found many mistakes and inconsistencies in almost every one of his biographies. As examples: In the life of Miltiades, he confounds Miltiades the son of Cimon, with Miltiades the son of Cypselus; in the life of Pausanius he confounds Darius and Xerxes; in the same biography he confounds the victory of Mycale, gained by Xanthippus, with the naval battle gained by Cimon, nine years after, near the river Eurymedon.

In the third chapter of the life of Lysander, Nepos confounds two expeditions of this general into Asia, between which there elapsed an interval of seven years.
In the second chapter of the life of Chabrias, utter confusion prevails.   At the period when Nepos makes
Agesilaus to have gone on his expedition into Egypt,
this monarch was busily occupied in Bœotia; and Nepos himself, in his life of Agesilaus, makes no mention
of this expedition.   The king of Egypt, who was assisted by Chabrias, was Tachos and not Nectanabis.
In the life of Hannibal, Cornelius makes that general
march to Rome directly, while it was not after the victory at Cannæ, but after having permitted the spirit
of his army to become corrupted in Campania, that
Hannibal directed his march toward Rome.   Many
other mistakes could be pointed out.   In regard to the
style and composition, the writings of Nepos are good.

C. Julius Cæsar was born in 100 B. C., of a family of
the Julian gens, one of the oldest among the patrician
families of Rome.   He became a soldier in the nineteenth year of his age, and his works display all the
best qualities which are fostered by military education
—frankness, simplicity, and brevity.   Cæsar had much
taste for eloquence, and he studied rhetoric and oratory
under a very able teacher, Apollonius Melos, who was
not only a teacher of rhetoric but also an able and eloquent pleader in the courts of law.   Cæsar showed his
talent for eloquence in several cases, but especially in
Catiline's conspiracy, when, without reason, he was suspected of having been an accomplice, and had to de-
fend himself.   In the year 63 he was appointed pontifex
maximus, and he examined diligently into the history

and nature of the Roman belief of the Auguri. He confined his remarks in a work, consisting of at least sixteen books, called "Libri Auspiciorum," which is lost. He studied astronomy, in order to fit himself for the discharge of his office, and even wrote a book, "De

JULIUS CÆSAR.

Astris." This led him to the reform of the calendar. Then Cæsar commenced his military career, during which he composed his "Commentaries," the only work extant from him. He wrote with his own hand seven books, containing the history of the seven years of the Gallic War; the eighth book was also commenced by him, and was finished by Hirtius, his most faithful companion and secretary. Three other books, also written by Cæsar, carry the history of the Civil War down to the Alexandrine.

These memoirs are exactly what they profess to be, and are written in the most appropriate style. They are sketches taken on the spot, in the midst of the action, while the mind is full; their elegance and polish show the least labored efforts of a refined and educated taste. The "Commentaries" are not so much a history as the materials for it. The calmness and equability of Cæsar's character pervade his writings; but these do not, for that reason, lack energy and life. Cicero says that the simple beauty of Cæsar's language is statuesque rather than picturesque. The "Commentaries" have been sometimes compared to Xenophon's writings; both are eminently simple and unaffected, but there the parallel ends. The first is stern, the second is sweet, and both are entirely different.

Cæsar had written other works, which are lost: 1. "The Anticatones," two books of answers to Cicero's panegyric on Cato; 2. "The Analogia," a sort of grammar of the Latin tongue, highly praised by Cicero; and, 3. His "Apophthegmata," a collection of wise sayings. He attempted to write poetry, and we know of 4. His "Œdipus," but we have the title only of this composition; 5. "Iter," an account of his march into Spain. We have spoken already of his astronomical poem. 6. Some "Epigrams," of which three are extant, although their authenticity is somewhat doubtful.

C. Sallustius Crispus, a native of Amiternum, in the territory of the Sabines, where he was born in 85. He was a member of a plebeian family, but he soon raised himself to the highest offices of the state. Sallust was sent away from the senate; why, it is doubtful. The character of Sallust has been greatly attacked both in regard to morality and honesty. As to the first point, it may be said that he was not any better than his contemporaries—the age was one of monstrous corruption —but sometimes his name has been mistaken for his nephew's, who bore the same, and was a monster of

SALLUST.

lust. In regard to his honesty, it is to be confessed that he acquired immense wealth in Numidia, where he remained for some time, having been appointed a governor of that province by Cæsar, after the defeat of the party of Pompey. That wealth, so ill-gotten, was used at Rome in the enjoyment of the greatest luxury. The gardens of the Quirinal, which bore the name of Sallust, were celebrated for their beauty, and the historian, beneath their alleys and porticos, sur-

rounded by the choicest works of art, avoided the
tumultuous scenes of civil war which were rending the
state at that time.

We have from Sallust " The History of the Conspiracy of Catiline," and of the war against Jugurtha.
Sallust evidently regarded fine style as one of the chief
merits of an historical work. His style was carefully
formed on that of Thucydides. He wonderfully succeeded in imitating the vigor and conciseness of the
Greek historian—we mean that he imitated the brevity of ideas, rather than of language, for Thucydides
is sometimes very diffuse; but Sallust is abrupt and
sententious, and he carried this brevity to a vicious
excess. The want of copulatives produces a monotonous effect.

In the style of Sallust there is too much appearance
of study, and a want of ease, which is the effect of art.
Sallust is a master in drawing his characters, five or six
of which are perfect. These are Cato, Cæsar, Catiline,
Jugurtha, Marius, and Sylla. Sallust sprinkles his
narrative with reflections, which are all very just, and
merit for him the appellation of the Father of Philosophic History in Italy. The discursive nature and
inordinate length of his introductions have been objected to, and with reason.

Besides these two histories, Sallust wrote a general
history of the republic—" Historia Rerum in Republica
Romana gestarum "—of which we have many, but too
short, fragments. The scholiasts and grammarians
have collected as many as seven hundred of them; the
only one of any length is the description of a splen-
did entertainment given to Metellus, on his return,

after a year's absence, from his government of Farther Spain.

Trogus Pompeius was a voluminous historian of the Augustan age, whose father was private secretary to Julius Cæsar. His work was of such an extent that it has been called by Justinus a universal history; but the title was "Historiæ Philippicæ," the object of which was evidently the history of the Macedonian monarchy. The work consists of forty-four books, the fragments of which we have, gathered into eight books by Justinus. They contain "The History of Alexander," unconnected, but interesting and well written.

T. Livius Patavinus was born in 59, at Padua (Patavinum). Although it is generally believed that Padua had the honor of being the birthplace of Livy, an epigram of Martial (book i., 52) has thrown some doubt upon the fact. Livy came to Rome very early; he wrote some poetry, and gained the favor of Augustus, who lodged him in his own palace. There he could consult for and prepare his work, the composition of which occupied him during twenty years. He soon acquired a great reputation. Late in life he returned to Patavinum, where he died in the year 17 after Christ, at the age of seventy-six years.

Some writer has said, and we think that he was right, that Livy was the Homer of the Roman people, on account of the epic color with which he has painted his characters, while the charm of his narrative makes him the Herodotus of Roman historians. The time when Livy was living was the most favorable for writing history. The great work of the formation of the Roman Empire was done. Livy could, owing to the peace which reigned for some time, consider and study that grand construction and describe it.

Livy published his work by portions; it comprehended the whole history of Rome from its foundation to the death of Drusus, the brother of Tiberius, 9 B. O. It consisted of one hundred and forty-two books, but only thirty-five are extant, with some fragments of the others. The first ten books, which we have, carry the history of Rome, from the arrival of Æneas in Italy, to the year 293 B. C., a few years before the war with Pyrrhus. There we have an hiatus of the following ten books. The narrative recommences at the twenty-first book, with the second Punic War, 218 B. O. We have there the whole history of Hannibal, and consequently the second Punic War, and the beginning of the third. It must be admitted that the best portion of Livy's history has perished, especially the part in connection with the time when he lived.

The abridgments of the books lost were collected by a learned German—Freinshemius—in the seventeenth century. This great Latinist, while imitating the style of Livy quite perfectly, reëstablished the whole work, with the best documents which he could find.

Tacitus and Seneca speak in the highest terms of the beauty of Livy's style, and the fidelity of his narrative. We may admit that his style is eloquent, his narrative clear, and his power of description great and striking. Some of his narratives are really perfect, like the one of the passage of the Alps by Hannibal. In regard to his fidelity, it cannot be denied that he was deficient in the first and most important requisites of a faithful historian—a love of truth, diligence and care in consulting authorities, and a patient examination of conflicting testimonies. Livy has made very little use of the documents and inscriptions which were within his reach, such as the brazen column in the Temple of the Aventine Diana, on which was engraven the treaty of Servius Tullius with the Latins, with the names of the tribes which were members of the league; the treaty of Tarquinius Superbus with Gabii, written on a bull's hide and preserved in the Temple of Dius Fidius, etc.

Livy does not found his narrative upon contemporary records, but avowedly draws his materials from the works of earlier annalists. As long as his guides agree in the main points of their history, he follows them; but, when they openly contradict each other, then he confesses the difficulty and acknowledges the uncertainty of the history of the first centuries of the city, and passes over these difficulties without a special notice. There are several proofs that he wrote carelessly and hastily. He sometimes repeats himself, and sometimes contradicts himself. He is not so much an historian as a poet. The love of Livy for his country may be noticed in the fact that never, in his history, have the Romans been defeated by their opponents!

Asinius Pollio has accused Livy of being guilty in his writings of *patavinity*, and Quintilian agrees, it seems, with Pollio. But, in what does this defect lie? Pollio says that there is something in Livy's expressions which bespeaks a citizen of Patavium, and which would not appear in the style of a native of

Rome. According to Quintilian, it applies entirely to provincial phrases and words not altogether consonant to the refined urbanity of Rome, which could not so easily be communicated to strangers as the freedom of the city.

The opinion of Beni, who supposes that—because the Patavians were all staunch republicans—the *patavinity* of Livy must have consisted in his political partiality to the faction of Pompey; and the one of Budæus, who thinks that Livy's *patavinity* lay in his enmity to the Gauls, who were the natural foes of the Patavians, are without foundation.

Some, at length, like Morhof and Laurentius Pignorius, pretend that this *patavinity* consists in a certain orthography peculiar to the Patavians—as *sibe* for *sibi*, *quase* for *quasi*—and in the diffuseness of style to which the Patavians, both ancient and modern, have been addicted in all their compositions. It is, at any rate, a very small matter.

M. Vitruvius Pollio.—We will only mention the work of this writer. It is a complete treatise on architecture, consisting of ten books. The subject is treated systematically and in an orderly style. Being a technical subject, it necessitated the introduction of new terms. There is in it much poverty of language, and some of the paraphrases are awkward, and the phraseology generally obscure. Still, upon the whole, the language of Vitruvius is vigorous, his descriptions bold, and the style generally correct, that is, grammatical.

Others wrote on architecture, but added nothing to the stock of their country's literature. So it was with the grammarians of the Augustan age, and consequently they may be passed over with the simple mention of their names. The most conspicuous were : **Atteius Philologus, Staberius Eros, Q. Cæcilius Epirota, C. Julius Hyginus,** the great friend of Ovid, **Verrius Flaccus, Q. Cornificius,** and **P. Nigidius Figulus,** an orator and philosopher as well as grammarian.

BOOK III.

THE SILVER AGE.

With the death of Augustus commences the decline of Roman literature, and only three illustrious names —Phædrus, Persius, and Lucian—rescue the first year of this period from the charge of a corrupt and vitiated taste. After several years of tyranny, a more liberal system of administration, under Vespasian, will allow Juvenal and Tacitus to resume the language of the old Roman independence. The characteristic of the first literature of this epoch was declamation and rhetoric, and this false taste, which destroys true natural eloquence, affected poetry as well as prose. Even in the tragedies which are ascribed to Seneca, we have but theatrical declamations.

CHAPTER I.

POETRY.

Section I.—Fables.

Phædrus was born in Thracia, and was brought to Rome, with other captives, after a victory gained by Octavius, the father of Augustus, over some Thracian

clans. Phædrus was then an infant, and he was reared
up among the slaves of Augustus. He calls himself a
freedman of Augustus—"Augusti libertus." In regard
to the place of his birth we know it by Phædrus himself, who, in the prologue of his third book, says:

"Ego quem Pierio mater enixa est jugo."

And again he adds:

"Ego literatæ qui sum proprior Græciæ,
   Cur somno inerti deseram patriæ decus;
   Threïssa cum gens numeret auctores suos,
   Linoque Apollo sit parens, Musa, Orpheo
   Qui saxa cantu movit, et domuit feras,
   Hebrique tenuit impetus dulci mora."

Phædrus wrote his "Fables" under the reign of
Tiberius, and while Sejanus had the administration of
the empire. He has the merit of having first made the
Romans acquainted with the fables of Æsop; but, in
the preface to his work, he modestly terms himself only
a translator of Æsop:

"Æsopus auctor quam materiam repperit
   Hanc ego polivi versibus senariis."

Still, his "Fables" are not mere translations, and
Phædrus undoubtedly deserves the credit of originality
for the way in which he has arranged them. Phædrus
wrote five books of fables, containing in all ninety
fables, written in iambic verse. He is distinguished
for a precision, gracefulness, and *naïveté* of style and
manner, that have never been surpassed. His diction
is remarkable for its elegance, though this occasionally
is pushed too far into the regions of refinement.

Phædrus was persecuted by Sejanus, and no wonder, when we consider the tyranny of that minister, and the meaning of the "Fables" of Phædrus, for in many of them it is easy to see that the fabulist was relating the events of the time under the veil of fables. This is true principally of the fables "The Frogs and the Sun," "The Mules and the Thieves," "The Old Peasant and the Ass," "The Man and the Ass," and "The Wolf and the Lamb."

Section II.—Satires.

Aulus Persius Flaccus was born in 34 B. C., at Volaterræ, in Etruria. He went to Rome when he was twelve years old, studied seriously, and was the schoolmate of Lucan. Persius was a Stoic, and a virtuous pagan. He died at the age of twenty-eight. His works consist of six "Satires," with a prologue, in all six hundred and fifty verses. The chief defect of Persius is an affected obscurity of style, which is so great and so general that there are few scholars who read these performances for the first time whose progress is not arrested at almost every line by some new difficulty. Much of this difficulty is owing to the peculiar character of the poet's mind, to his affected conciseness, and to the show of erudition which he is so fond of exhibiting. In the following verses we may see the honest sentiments which animated Persius. Even a Christian can read them with admiration:

"Quin damus id superis, de magna quod dare lance
  Non possit magni Messalæ lippa propago;
  Compositum jus fasque animo sanctosque recessus
  Mentis et incoctum generoso pectus honesto:
  Hæc cedo, ut admoveam templis, et farre litabo."

Decius Junius Juvenalis (some write Decimus Junius) was born at Aquinum, in the town which subsequently gave birth to the eminent schoolman Thomas
Aquinas. The year of his birth is not certainly known,
but it is commonly believed that he was born in the
year 40 after Christ. A great portion of Juvenal's life
was passed during a period of political horror and
misery. For some reason not well known, but probably on account of some allusion made in one of his
satires to some favorite of the emperor, Juvenal, when
he was eighty years old, was sent, under the false pre-
text of taking a delusory command, to Egypt, by the
Emperor Adrian, and some say that he died there,
while some writers pretend that he was called back to
Rome, where he died in 128, at the age of eighty-eight
years.

We have sixteen "Satires" from the pen of Juvenal. If we may judge of the character of a writer
by his work, Juvenal was a man of rigid probity, and
worthy of living in a better and purer age. His
"Satires" breathe everywhere a love of virtue and
an abhorrence of vice. He paints in strong colors the
hypocrisy and the vices of the pretended philosophers
of his time. He found the weapons for attacking them
in the resources of his own genius, by the experience
which a long acquaintance with the world had gained
for him, and by the indignation which warmed his
bosom on contemplating the gross corruption of his
time. Juvenal has been compared to Horace. He is
superior to this last writer in this sense, that he is more
of a satirist, for, like Horace, he does not laugh at
vices, but speaks with indignation against them; and,

besides, the writings of Juvenal are addressed to the encouragement of virtue no less than to the chastisement of vice. The style of Juvenal is vigorous and lucid, although he fell into the defect common to the writers of that epoch; he is declamatory in his style, but not artificially rhetorical. He may be blamed for sometimes using language gross and offensive, but it was on account of the nature of the subject which he was treating. The "Satires" of Juvenal might be recommended to youth, if they did not descend so minutely into the details of vice.

Section III.—Epic Style.

M. Annæus Lucanus, born at Corduba, in 39 after Christ, was of a Roman family of equestrian rank. He went early to Rome and studied grammar, rhetoric, and philosophy, embracing the principles of Zeno. Lucan soon discovered his talent for poetry. He was a friend of the Emperor Nero, but, having committed the imprudence of showing his superiority over him, he offended his master, and that was the cause of his death, which took place when he was only twenty-seven years old. The following inscription to his memory has been attributed to Nero:

"M. Annæo Lucano, Cordubensi Poëtae,
Beneficio Neronis.   Fama servata."

Besides his "Pharsalia" he composed four poems, viz.: "Combat of Hector and Achilles," "Description of the Burning of Rome," "Saturnalia," and a tragedy called "Medea." They are not now extant. "The Pharsalia" is the history of the war between Cæsar and Pompey; it comprises ten books, and very probably it is not finished. This poem contains many vigorous and animated descriptions, and the speeches are characterized by considerable rhetorical merit, but the language is often inflated, and the expressions are extremely labored and artificial. The poem, although of an epic character, should rather be called an historical poem, for the event was not sufficiently removed from Lucan's time to permit him to indulge in those fictions which belong to the essence of the epopee. The principal defect of "The Pharsalia" is the want of unity of action. It is really impossible, on perusing it, to ascertain the object of the poet. His principal heroes are Cæsar and Pompey, and Cato and Brutus. In the delineation of these characters Lucan is defective, Pompey is flattered, and Cæsar is treated with injustice. However, Lucan did not succeed in making the first interesting, Cæsar being, after all, the true hero. Many of the details show a want of taste, but we ought not to forget that Lucan was young. The versification also wants the elegance and melody of Virgil. Some passages of "The Pharsalia" are beautiful; the description of the passage of the Rubicon, and the death of Pompey, are noble specimens of Lucan's style.

The following extract will give a sufficient idea of Lucan's poetry. A parallel is established between Pompey and Cæsar:

"Nec quemquam jam ferre potest, Cæsarve priorem,
  Pompeiusve parem. Quis justius induit arma?
  Scire nefas; magno se judice quisque tuetur.
  Victria causa diis placuit, sed victa Catoni.

9

Nec coiere pares. Alter vergentibus armis
In senium, longoque togæ tranquillior usu,
Dedidicit jam pace ducem; famæque petitor,
Multa dare in vulgus, totus popularibus auris
Impelli, plausuque sui gaudere theatri,
Nec reparare novas vires, multumque priori
Credere fortunæ: stat magni nominis umbra.
Qualis frugifero quercus sublimis in agro
Exuvias veteres populi, sacrataque gestans
Dona ducum, nec jam validis radicibus hærens,
Pondere fixa suo est, nudosque per aera ramos
Effundens, trunco, non frondibus, efficit umbram:
At quamvis primo nutet casura sub Euro,
Tot circum sylvæ firmo se robore tollant,
Sola tamen colitur. Sed non in Cæsare tantum
Nomen erat, nec fama ducis; sed nescia virtus
Stare loco, solusque pudor non vincere bello.
Acer et indomitus; quo spes, quoque ira vocasset,
Ferre manum, et nunquam temerando parcere ferro;
Successus urgere suos; instare favore
Numinis, impellens quidquid sibi summa petenti
Obstaret, gaudensque viam fecisse ruina.
Qualiter expressum ventis per nubila fulmen,
Ætheris impulsi sonitu mundique fragore
Emicuit, rupitque diem, populosque paventes
Terruit, obliqua perstringens lumina flamma:
In sua templa furit, nullaque exire vetante
Materia, magnamque cadens, magnamque revertens
Dat stragem late, sparsosque recolligit ignes."

C. Silius Italicus was born most probably in Spain, in 25 after Christ, under the reign of Tiberius. He was a very celebrated advocate; in the year 68 he became consul, and soon after was sent to Asia as a proconsul, and during the time that he was in office acted very honestly. Silius grew very rich, and, when he was old, he retired from public life. He starved himself to death at the age of seventy-five years, being unable to bear the sufferings which he was enduring on account of a carbuncle. His poems display elaborate care rather than genius. The title of the work which we have is "Punica," the dullest and most tedious poem in the Latin language; it contains seventeen books, and gives the history of the second Punic War. "The Æneïs" was his model, and the writings of Livy furnished the materials. The criticism of Pliny is just: "Scribebat carmina majori cura quam ingenio." Although it is impossible to read his poem as a whole with pleasure, the versification is harmonious, and, in point of smoothness, sometimes bears comparison with that of Virgil. Silius describes well, and some of his episodes, considered as separate pieces, repay the trouble of perusal; we may point out the description of the Alps as a model.

C. Valerius Flaccus, who flourished under Vespasian, was born at Rome, and died in 88. His only poem extant is entitled "Argonautica," and is an imitation of the Greek poem of Apollonius Rhodius on the same subject. He did not live to complete the work; even the eighth book remains unfinished, and, judging from what we have, he planned a poem of the same length as that of Virgil. There are in this work no glaring faults or blemishes. There is some occasional dryness, and a few awkward expressions and paraphrases, but there is no bombast to outrage good taste, nor unmetrical cadences to offend the ear; on the other hand, there is no genius, no inspiration, no thrilling fervor, no thoughts that breathe nor words that burn. He never rises above the dead level; every thing is in accordance with decent and correct propriety; he describes well, and his verses are harmonious.

P. Papinius Statius, the Younger, was born at Naples, in 61, and died in the same city when he was 34 years old. Statius possessed a ready facility for versification, which was surpassed by no one in classic antiquity but Ovid, and he was successful as long as he contented himself with being a poet on a small scale. His principal productions were "The Sylvæ," "The Achilleid," and "The Thebaid." "The Sylvæ" consist of thirty-two separate pieces, and they contain many poetical incidents which might stand by themselves as fugitive pieces. It matters not how light or trifling the subject may be, he can raise it and adorn it. He writes with equal beauty on the tree of his friend Atedius (Sylv. ii., 5), the death of a parrot, of the emperor's lion (Sylv. ii., 3), the locks of Flavius Earinus (Sylv. ii., 4), etc. The principal fault of his "Silvæ" is too great a display of Greek learning. Every page is full of mythological allusions, which sometimes render his graceful verses dry and wearisome. The qualities which recommend his "Sylvæ" do not adorn his epic poetry; his imaginary heroes do not inspire and warm his imagination, and he attempts to compensate for this deficiency by extravagant bombast, and by an attention to the theoretical principles of art and an elaborate finish. He owes the estimation in which he is held as an epic poet to his relative merit; he was the best of the heroic poets of his day. Statius was evidently a profound student, and in two points, that is, in his battles and similes, he has shown himself a successful imitator of Homer. "The Thebaid" is composed of twelve books, and its subject is the ancient Greek legends respecting the war of the Seven against Thebes. "The Achilleid" was intended to embrace the exploits of Achilles; but two books only were completed, the second even being unfinished.

Domitian.—This emperor also wrote verses, and not without merit in regard to language and versification. We have from him a paraphrase of "The Phænomena" of Aratus, falsely ascribed to Germanicus; it is written with taste, but Domitian had not much talent.

Section IV.—Epigrams.

M. Valerius Martialis was born in Spain, at Bilbilis, in the province of Tarragon, in the year 43. The Emperor Vespasian having conferred the "jus Latii" on his native place, Martial was by birth a Roman citizen. He came to Rome when he was twenty-two years old, in the twelfth year of the reign of Nero. He was a great favorite of Titus and Domitian, and, although he complains of his poverty, he was rich enough. Martial lived thirty-five years in Rome, and was a flatterer all the time He then returned to his native place, and married a rich widow, whom he praised beyond expression in his writings, and, when inclined to regret, he says that she alone is all that Rome ever was to him:

"Tu desiderium dominæ mihi mitius urbis
Esse jubes; Romam tu mihi sola facis."

Notwithstanding his assertion, Martial regretted much having left Rome. He died in 104, and left twelve hundred "Epigrams," forming fourteen books. These epigrams are not, with Martial, harmless verses, but they are essentially satirical compositions. His "Epigrams" reveal in a strong, and too unveiled language, the fearful profligacy of his time. He speaks of it with a cynical delight. This would be a crime in our time, but the prevalence of vice at that epoch produced the obscenity of the poet. This is, however, the only defence we may offer for his works, in which the characters of vice are emblazoned in such shameless and unnatural deformity. It is difficult, when we read Martial, to believe what he says, that, although his verses are licentious, his life was virtuous:

" Lasciva est nobis pagina, vita proba est."

We observe in Martial that strange combination of varied wit, poetical imagination, and graceful language, not only with strong passions, but with a delight in vice in its most hateful form and attributes. All his poems are not thus spiteful and obscene; some are redolent of Greek sweetness and elegance, like the following lines accompanying a rose to Apollinaris:

"I, felix rosa, mollibusque sertis
 Nostri cinge comas Apollinaris;
 Quas tu nectere candidas sed olim,
 Sic te semper amet Venus, memento."

Here is another favorable specimen of his poetry:

"Indignas premeret pestis cum tabida fauces,
 Inque ipsos vultus serperet atra lues;
 Siccis ipse genis flentes hortatus amicos
 Decrevit stygios Festus adire lacus.
 Nec tamen obscuro pia polluit ora veneno,
 Aut torsit lenta tristia fata fame;
 Sanctam Romana vitam sed morte peregit,
 Dimisitque animam nobiliore via.
 Hanc mortem fatis magni præferre Catonis
 Fama potest; hujus Cæsar amicus erat."

CHAPTER II.

PROSE—HISTORY.

Velleius Paterculus was a soldier of equestrian rank under Tiberius, and probably was put to death after the fall of Sejanus. He wrote a short "History of Rome," in two books. The first is in a very imperfect state, but the second is well preserved. It is a work of much merit; the most striking events are selected, and told in a lively and interesting manner. Unfortunately, Paterculus is partial, prejudiced, and adulatory. He was a man of lively talents, although of superficial education, and his language shows already signs of degeneracy in the Latin tongue. In his style he imitates the concise and energetic manner of Sallust. His diction is generally pure and elegant, but he falls into affectations by searching for archaisms and antiquated forms of expression, and by using too frequently moral sentences and figures of rhetoric. Paterculus also draws his characters with a masterly hand.

Valerius Maximus lived at the same time as Paterculus, and can scarcely be called an historian. He wrote a collection of anecdotes entitled "Dictorum, Factorum Memorabilium Libri IX." His purpose is a moral one, and he wants to illustrate by examples the beauty of virtue and the deformity of vice. Nothing is known for certain respecting his personal history. His work is dedicated to Tiberius. He classifies the individuals of whom he treats according to some peculiar vice or virtue, of which they are cited as examples. Valerius, in the whole work, displays very little judgment; no one ever carried flattery to a greater extent. His manner of narration is far from pleasing, and his style is cold, declamatory, and affected.

C. Cornelius Tacitus was born probably in the year 54, but it is not exactly known. He was of equestrian rank, and, under the reigns of Vespasian and Titus, he was procurator of Belgic Gaul. In the year 78, he

TACITUS.

married the daughter of Agricola. Tacitus discharged several high offices in the state. It is not known when Tacitus died, nor whether he left any descendants; but, no doubt, he survived the accession of Hadrian.

The works of Tacitus are extensive. We have from him: 1. A life of his father-in-law, Agricola; 2. A treatise on "The Manners, Situation, and Nations of the Germans;" 3. A portion of a voluminous work entitled "Histories;" 4. About two-thirds of another historical work called "Annales;" and, 5. According to the most probable opinion, a dialogue on "The Decline of Eloquence." The brief sketch of the life of

Agricola is a beautiful specimen of the vigor and force of expression with which this greatest painter of antiquity could throw off any portrait which he attempted. The treatise on " The Geography, Manners, and Nations of the Germans " (De Situ, Moribus et Populis Germaniæ), is but little longer than the life of Agricola. Tacitus was never in Germany; his knowledge is consequently collected from those who had visited it, for the purpose either of war or commerce. Hence his geographical descriptions are sometimes vague and inaccurate, still the salient points of the national manners bear the impress of truth. We have four books of his "Historiæ," and a portion of the fifth, from the second consulship of Galba to the siege of Jerusalem. According to St. Jerome the work consisted of thirty books; these books are a vast field of faithful history, and the few blots—which, indeed, are few—come from the too great readiness of Tacitus to accept evidence unhesitatingly. The "Annals " are so called because each historical event is recorded in historical order, under the year in which it belongs. They consist of sixteen books, commence with the death of Augustus, and conclude with that of Nero. The only portions extant are the first four books, a part of the fifth, the sixth, a part of the eleventh, and then the twelfth, thirteenth, fourteenth, fifteenth, and commencement of the sixteenth. They are rather histories of each successive emperor than of the Roman people. Tacitus delineated the lives and deaths of individuals, and showed the relation which they bore to the fortunes of their country.

Full of observation and descriptive power, Tacitus

engages the serious attention of the reader by the gravity of his condensed and comprehensive style, as he does by the wisdom and earnestness of his reflections. In the style of Tacitus the form is always subordinate to the matter. His brevity is the necessary condensation of a writer whose thoughts flow more quickly than his pen can express them. That brevity is neither dry nor harsh; it is enlivened by copiousness, variety, and poetry. He scarcely ever repeats the same idea in the same form; no author is richer in synonymous words. As for poetic genius, his language is highly figurative; his descriptions are eminently picturesque. The discourses found in the writings of Tacitus show that he was not only a good historian but also a perfect orator, and that he deserved the praise given him by Pliny the Younger.

Suetonius Tranquillus was the son of Suetonius Lenis, a tribune in the army which fought at Bedriacum, and was born at the beginning of the reign of Vespasian (71), but the precise date of his birth is not known. He followed at Rome the profession of grammarian. Pliny obtained for him the favors of Trajan. Suetonius wrote twelve "Biographies" of the first twelve Cæsars. These were Julius Cæsar, Augustus, Tiberius, Caligula, Claudius, Nero, Galba, Otho, Vitellius, Vespasian, Titus, and Domitian. His purpose was to delineate their private character, their virtues, and vices. His narrative does not follow a chronological order. The characters are faithfully traced. He, like Plutarch, gathered his materials from several very different authorities, but these authorities were better known to him than were to Plutarch those which have been used by him. His style is simple, concise, and correct, without ornament or affectation. We have from Suetonius an account of distinguished grammarians, and of celebrated rhetoricians. He wrote other books which are not extant.

Q. Curtius Rufus.—No ancient writer speaks of him, and it is only in the twelfth century that he is mentioned. From one passage only of his writings we may form some conjecture concerning the time when he lived—it was very likely under Vespasian. His book is entitled "De Rebus Gestis Alexandri Magni." It was divided into ten books, but the first two, the end of the fifth, and the beginning of the sixth, are lost. Freinshemius has done for him what he did for Livy— he has completed the work. The history of Q. Curtius is more of a romance than a history. The speeches which Rufus puts in the mouths of his heroes are mere rhetorical declamations. Giving the history of Alexander from documents, Rufus chose those which pleased him the most, not paying attention to the purity of the sources. He shows everywhere his ignorance of military affairs, of geography and astronomy, and confounds many things. We might compare the book of Q. Curtius to "The History of Charles XII.," by Voltaire; it is done evidently for the purpose not of writing history, but of writing. Surely, if Curtius be not an historian, he is a very interesting writer. His diction is pure and elegant, some of his harangues are masterpieces, and he is rich in beautiful descriptions. His style has the defect generally found in the "Silver Age," being too ornamented, and sometimes declamatory.

L. Annæus Florus was born either in Spain or in Gaul,

and he wrote under the reign of Trajan. We can give nothing more precise concerning the time and the place of his birth. He has left an abridgment of Roman history, entitled "Epitome de Gestis Romanorum," from the foundation of Rome to the year 725, when Augustus shut the Temple of Janus. It is less a history than a eulogium of the Roman people, written with elegance, but with affectation. Florus committed many faults in a geographical and chronological point of view. His text has reached us in a very corrupt state, and abounds with interpolations. It has been said that the work was from Seneca, but this opinion cannot be accepted; besides, we know that Seneca belonged to a branch of the Annæan family, and Florus may have been called Seneca, or some mistake may have been committed by the copyist.

CHAPTER III.

PROSE—PHILOSOPHERS AND GRAMMARIANS.

M. Annæus Seneca was born at Cordova, in the year 61 B. C. He was the father of L. Annæus Seneca the Philosopher. He left two works, the composition of which was the employment of his old age. They are the result of his long and successful experience as a teacher of rhetoric. They exhibit wit, learning, ingenuity, and taste to select and admire the best literary specimens of earlier periods. The first work was entitled "Controversiæ," and was divided into ten books, of which the first, second, seventh, eighth, and tenth, are extant. His other work, "The Suasoriæ," contains exercises in deliberative oratory, the subjects of which are taken from the historians and poets.

L. Annæus Seneca, the son of the former, was born at Cordova, at the commencement of the Christian era. His father brought him to Rome when he was young, and there he studied rhetoric and philosophy. He had a very stormy life, under the reign of Claudius, when he was exiled to Corsica on account of a calumny.

SENECA.

After eight years he was recalled to Rome, to be the preceptor of Nero. The pupil was vicious, and Seneca did not see that it was his duty to try seriously to correct him; he only endeavored to gain the favor of his pupil. Seneca, by usury and legacy-hunting, had acquired one of those enormous fortunes of which so many instances are met with in Roman history. He incurred subsequently the displeasure of Nero, although, in order to comply with the wickedness of that monster, he had denied the culpability of Nero in the death of his mother, and even made the apology of the parricide. He was put to death, or rather he had to kill himself.

Seneca is the author of twelve ethical treatises, the best of which are entitled "De Providentia," "De Constantia Sapientis," and "De Consolatione." In the treatise "De Providentia" he discusses the question, "Why, since there is a divine Providence, are good men liable to misfortunes?" and Seneca finds that there is a legitimate remedy, when the sum of evil is greater than that of good, and that is suicide. Seneca cared little for abstract speculations; he valued them only as subordinate to mental and natural philosophy. He delighted in inculcating precepts rather than investigating principles, and, for that reason, his works furnish a rich mine for quotations. Seneca was always a favorite with Christian writers—some of his sentiments are truly Christian; there is even a tradition · that he was acquainted with St. Paul, and fourteen letters of that apostle have been attributed to him. His "Epistles," of which there are one hundred and twenty-four, are moral essays in an epistolary form, and are the most delightful of his works.

In his old age, he wrote seven books on questions connected with natural phenomena — "Quæstionum Naturalinm Libri VII.;" but Seneca treats those subjects like a moralist, and makes them the occasion of ethical reflections. He wrote one satire, "The Funeral Oration of Claudius." Seneca wrote also seven tragedies; although six of them have been attributed by some grammarians to his father, and it has even been said that they were the work of another Seneca—a third one—it seems well demonstrated to-day that L. Annæus Seneca the Philosopher was the author of those tragedies.   They are: "Medea," "Troades," "Hippolytus," "Agamemnon," "Hercules Fureus," "Thyestes," and "Hercules in Œta."   As to these compositions, it is really impossible to find a good tragedy among them.   All are defective in plan, and in the management of the pieces; they are all barren of action, and full of declamation.   They are modelled after Greek tragedies, but are very far from being good copies.   They generally embody the ethical philosophy of Seneca.   The style of Seneca is the one which characterizes best the style of the "Silver Age." It is faulty, like the style of Juvenal, and Tacitus, and Lucan; that means that it is beyond the pale of the best Latinity.   Quintilian and Aulus Gellius have criticised it too severely.   Seneca was a good writer, but he had the defect, as we have said, common to the writers of his time: he was too declamatory, too fond of sparkle and glitter. · He might be compared, for his love of antithesis, to Victor Hugo.

· **C. Plinius Secundus**, the Elder, was born in 23, at Verona, or Como.   He received his education in Rome, and served in Germany under Claudius; then he returned to Rome, and practised at the bar, filled different civil offices, and was subsequently procurator in Spain.   A letter of his nephew tells us of his passion for study, and makes us acquainted with the details of his death—which happened at the time of the first eruption of Mount Vesuvius, in 79—and with his works.

Plinius the Naturalist wrote: 1. "The Art of Using the Javelin on Horseback;" 2. "The Life of Pomponius Secundus;" 3. "A History of the Twenty Wars carried on by the Romans with the Germans;" 4. "A Treatise on Eloquence;" 5. Eight books on "Grammatical Ambiguity;" 6. Thirty books of "History;" and 7. Thirty-seven books on "Natural History." This work is an unequalled monument of studious diligence and persevering industry; it consists of thirty-seven books, and contains twenty thousand facts connected with Nature and art. There is in it, of course, a confused arrangement; but it is owing to the indefinite state of science, and the mixture of branches which are separate and distinct. Pliny admits too easily many tales which even are absurd, but we find in the work many valuable truths. The style is always full of vigor and expression, but sometimes too florid and bombastic. The philosophical character of the whole work is pantheistic. Pliny was only fifty-six years old when he died, and, of all his writings, only the "Natural History" has come down to us.

C. Plinius Cæcilius Secundus, the Younger, was sister's son to the elder Pliny. He was born in 61, at Como, and was eighteen years old when the eruption above mentioned took place. He was well educated, and had for his teacher of grammar Quintilian. His taste for literature was cultivated early, and he wrote verses, although his prose only remains. The works of Pliny are, "The Panegyric of Trajan," and ten books of very valuable letters—valuable on account of the information which they give about the manners and modes of thought of his time, and the politics of the day.   They are most delightful to read, and are not inferior to those of Cicero for liveliness, descriptive power, elegance, and simplicity of style.   In one

PLINY.

of them we have a "Biography of Silius Italicus," a very important document.   We give it as an example of Pliny's style:

DE INGENIO, VITA ET MORIBUS SILII ITALICI, CUJUS OBITUS DOCET QUÆ SIT HUMANÆ VITÆ FRAGILITAS.

"Modo nuntiatus est Silius Italicus in Neapolitano suo inedia vitam finisse. Causa mortis, valetudo. Erat illi natus insanabilis clavus, cujus tædio ad mortem irrevocabili constantia decucurrit: usque ad supremum diem beatus et felix, nisi quod minorem ex liberis duobus amisit; sed majorem melioremque, florentem atque etiam consularem reliquit. Læserat famam suam sub Nerone; credebatur sponte accusasse. Sed in Vitellii amicitia sapienter se et comiter gesserat; ex proconsulatu Asiæ gloriam reportaverat: maculam veteris industriæ laudabili otio

abluerat. Fuit inter principes civitatis sine potentia, sine invidia.
Salutabatur, colebatur, multumque in lectulo jacens, cubiculo semper non ex fortuna frequenti. Doctissimis sermonibus dies trans-
igebat, quum a scribendo vacaret. Scribebat carmina majore
cura quam ingenio: nonnunquam judicia hominum recitationibus
experiebatur. Novissime, ita suadentibus annis, ab urbe secessit,
seque in Campania tenuit; ac ne adventu quidem novi principis
inde commotus est. Magna Cæsaris laus, sub quo hoc liberum
fuit; magna illius qui hac libertate ausus est uti. Erat φιλόκαλος *
usque ad emacitatis reprehensionem. Plures iisdem in locis villas
possidebat, adamatisque novis, priores negligebat. Multum ubique
librorum, multum statuarum, multum imaginum, quas non habe-
bat modo, verum etiam venerabatur; Virgilii ante omnes, cujus
natalem religiosius quam suum celebrabat, Neapoli maxime, ubi
monumentum ejus adire, ut templum, solebat. In hac tranquilli-
tate annum quintum et septuagesimum excessit, delicato magis
corpore quam infirmo. Utque novissimus a Nerone factus est
consul, ita postremus ex omnibus quos Nero consules fecerat, de-
cessit. Illud etiam notabile; ultimus ex Neronianis consularibus
obiit, quo consule Nero periit. Quod me recordantem, fragilitatis
humanæ miseratio subit. Quid enim tam circumcisum, tam breve,
quam hominis vita longissima? An non videtur tibi Nero modo
fuisse, quum interim ex iis qui sub illo gesserant consulatum, nemo
jam superest? Quanquam quid hoc miror? Nuper Lucius Piso,
pater Pisonis illius qui a Valerio Festo per summum facinus in
Africa occisus est, dicere solebat, *Neminem se videre in senatu,
quem consul ipse sententiam rogavisset.* Tam angustis terminis
tantæ multitudinis vivacitas ipsa concluditur, ut mihi non venia
solum dignæ, verum etiam laude videantur illæ regiæ lacrymæ.
Nam ferunt Xerxem, quum immensum exercitum oculis obiisset,
illacrymasse, quod tot millibus tam brevis immineret occasus.
Sed tanto magis hoc, quidquid est temporis futilis et caduci, si
non datur factis (nam horum materia in aliena manu), nos certe
studiis proferamus; et, quatenus nobis denegatur diu vivere, re-
linquamus aliquid, quo nos vixisse testemur. Scio te stimulis non
egere; me tamen tui charitas evocat, ut currentem quoque in-

* Rerum pulchrarum cupidus.

stigem, sicut tu soles me. 'Αγαθὴ δ' ἔρις * quum invicem se mu-
tuis exhortationibus amici ad amorem immortalitatis exacuunt.
Vale."

The tenth book is the most important, containing
the letters of Pliny to Trajan, and several answers of
that prince. · Pliny died in 110, at the age of forty-
nine years.

M. Fabius Quintilianus was born in Spain in 42, and
died at Rome in 118. He went there early, and was
twenty years a teacher of grammar and rhetoric. He
had Pliny the Younger as a pupil, and also two grand-
nephews of the Emperor Domitian. Quintilian was
paid by the state; he was in good circumstances, although he could not at that time be called a rich man.
He married twice.

His countryman Martial, speaking of him as the
glory of the Roman bar, and the head of his profession
as an instructor, says:

> " Quintiliane, vagæ moderator summe juventæ,
>   Gloria Romanæ, Quintiliane, togæ."

Quintilian's great work is entitled "Institutiones
Oratoriæ," in twelve books. It is a complete treatise
on the rhetorical art, which embraces a plan of study
for the orator from the first elements of grammar.
Quintilian here states the results of long experience
and deep reflection. He gives signal proofs in it of an
excellent judgment, of a refined, critical spirit, of a pure
taste, and of extensive and varied reading. This work
is preferable to all that we have from Cicero respect-

---

* Bona autem concertatio, hæc mortalibus.—HESIODUS.

ing the theory of eloquence. Quintilian has formed his style upon that of Cicero, and he writes with an elegance which would entitle him to rank by the side of the present models of the Augustan age, if certain obscure expressions, and some specimens of affected phraseology, did not betray a later writer. His tenth book contains a very precious " History of Ancient Literature." The declamations ascribed to him do not, certainly, belong to Quintilian.

The disposition of Quintilian was as affectionate and tender as his genius was brilliant and his taste pure. Few passages, throughout the whole range of Latin literature, can be compared to that in which he mourns the loss of his wife and children. We may judge by the following translation :

" I had a son," says he, " whose eminent genius deserved a father's anxious diligence. I thought that if—which I might fairly have expected and wished for —if death had removed me from him, I could have left him, as the best inheritance, a father's instructions. But by a second blow, a second bereavement, I have lost the object of my highest hopes, the only comfort of my declining years. What shall I do now? Of what use can I suppose myself to be, as the gods have cast me off? It happened that when I commenced my book on the causes of corrupt eloquence, I was stricken by a similar blow. It would have been best then to have flung myself upon the funeral-pile—which was destined prematurely to consume all that bound me to life—my unlucky work, and the ill-starred fruits of all my toils, and not to have wearied with new cares a life to which I so unnaturally clung. For what tender parent would pardon me if I were able to study any longer, and not hate my firmness of mind, if I, who survived all my dear ones, could find any employment for my tongue, except to accuse the gods, and to protest that no Providence looks down upon the affairs of men ?

" Their mother had before been torn from me, who had given birth to two sons before she had completed her nineteenth year ; and, though her death was a cruel blow to me, to her it was a happy one. To me the affliction was so crushing that Fortune could no longer restore me to happiness. For not only did the exercise of every feminine virtue render her husband's grief incurable, but, compared with my own age, she was but a girl, and therefore her loss may be accounted as that of a child. Still my children survived, and were my joy and comfort, and she, since I survived, escaped by a precipitate flight the agonies of grief. In my younger son, who died at five years old, I lost one light of my eyes. I have no ambition to make much of my misfortunes, or to exaggerate the reasons which I have for sorrow ; would that I had means of assuaging it! But how can I conceal his lovely countenance, his endearing talk, his sparkling wit, and (what I feel can scarcely be believed) his calm and deep solidity of mind ? Had he been another's child, he would have won my love. But insidious Fortune, in order to inflict on me severer anguish, made him more affectionate to me than to his nurses, his grandmother, who brought him up, and all who generally gain the attachment of children of that age.

" Thankful, therefore, do I feel for that sorrow in

which but a few months before I was plunged by the loss of his matchless, his inestimable mother; one only hope, support, and consolation, had remained in my Quintilian. He had not, like my younger son, just put forth his early blossoms, but, entering on his tenth year, had shown mature and well-set fruit. In him I discerned such vigor of intellect, such a zeal for study, which never required pressing, but also such uprightness, filial affection, refinement, and generosity, as furnished grounds for apprehending the thunder-stroke which has fallen. He possessed also those gifts which are accidental—a clear and melodious voice, a sweet pronunciation, a correct enunciation of every letter both in Greek and Latin; he possessed also the far higher qualities of constancy, earnestness, and firmness to bear sorrow and to resist fear. O dearest object of my disappointed hopes! could I behold thy glazing eyes, thy fleeting, when life began to fail! could I embrace thy cold and lifeless form, and live to drink again the common air! Well do I deserve these agonizing thoughts, these tortures which I endure!"

It is the touching eloquence of one who could not write otherwise than gracefully.

Aurelius Cornelius Celsus, a physician, who lived probably under the reign of Tiberius. The only work extant from him is a treatise, in eight books, on medicine, written in a beautiful Augustan style, and showing the learning of Celsus as a physician. The best evidence of the merit of the book of this writer is that, in our days, it is yet a text-book found in the hands of many pupils of medicine. He has been called the Cicero Medicorum.

Another physician, SCRIBONIUS LARGUS DESIGNATI-ANUS, was the author of several works, one of which, a large collection of prescriptions, is extant.

Pomponius Mela wrote, under the reign of Claudius, a geographical book, "De Situ Orbis Libri III." The book is systematic and learned. The simplicity of the style, and almost Augustan purity of the Latinity, prevent so bare a skeleton and list of facts from being dry and uninteresting.

L. Junius Moderatus Columella wrote a didactic work, "De Re Rustica," in twelve books, the tenth of which is written in verse; it is rather metrical prose than poetry, but the versification is correct, and the whole work, which is well composed, shows great fluency. Nothing is known of his life.

Sextus Julius Frontinus deserves a place among the Roman classical writers for his two books now extant. The first is on military tactics, and entitled "Strategematica Libri IV." It is a good composition, and a very valuable work to the antiquarian, although of no practical utility to the tactician. The other work, which we have complete, is a descriptive architectural treatise, in two books. Besides those two works, we have fragments of other writings, one of which is on surveying—"Agri Mensores," or "Rei Agrariæ Scriptores." They were scientific and jurisprudential at the same time.

Frontinus occupied several offices in the city, under the Emperor Vespasian. He was even sent to succeed Cerialis, as governor of Britain, by this same emperor. He died in the year 106.

With Frontinus ends the list of the classical writers

in the Latin language.　After him we have many authors, but few of them could imitate the literature of the Augustan age.　The brightest stars which illuminated the darkness were Aulus Gellius, Appuleius, Petronius, Lactantius, and the first Christian writers.

APPENDIX.

ALTHOUGH in the body of our work we have given the names of the principal writers who belong to the period of *Greek classical literature,* still we have deemed it well to insert, by way of appendix, a short notice of a few authors of a much later era, but whose works nevertheless are, on account of their intrinsic merit, justly numbered among the classics, and, as such, read in many schools and colleges.

As the first of this number we may mention **Theocritus,** the most celebrated of bucolic poets, who flourished at Syracuse, in Sicily, B. C. 270. In his youth he received instructions under able masters. Subsequently he became a friend of Aratus, a Greek poet of Cilicia, and lived part of his time at Alexandria, and the rest at Syracuse. The circumstances of his death are not precisely known, but it has been supposed, without sufficient reason, however, that he was strangled by order of Hiero, King of Sicily, in revenge for some pieces of a satirical nature which the poet had written against him. Theocritus is distinguished chiefly for his bucolic poems, all of which were written in the Dorian dialect.

Fifty-one poems are attributed to him, thirty of which—belonging to the bucolic order—are entitled "Idyls," and the remainder "Epigrams." Theocritus has had many imitators, both among the ancients and moderns, but in grace and *naïveté* of diction he stands yet unrivalled. He is sometimes indelicate in his expressions, but otherwise his works are faithful copies of nature,

10

characterized by a picturesque description of scenery, and a richness and delicacy of fancy rarely to be met with in any other
author.

Lucian, a distinguished writer, born at Samosata, in Syria,
lived several centuries later than Theocritus, but is notwithstanding justly entitled to a prominent place among the classic authors
of Greek literature. The age in which he flourished is not known,
but it is generally believed that he lived about the time of Trajan,
although many are of opinion that he was of a much later date.
He was at first an advocate at Antioch, but, having relinquished
this profession, he devoted himself to literary pursuits, in which
he soon attained great celebrity. He had a particular love for
travel, and at an early age visited Greece, Asia, and Gaul, and in
this last-mentioned country he remained in the capacity of teacher
of rhetoric, until he was about forty years of age. After leaving
Gaul he visited Italy, and many other countries, particularly the
provinces of Greece and Asia Minor. He lived, however, a greater
part of his time in Athens, where he died, at a very advanced age.
He wrote numerous works on various subjects, the greater part
of which were in the form of dialogue. They were nearly all of
a satirical nature, and were directed against the prevailing vices
and follies of the day.

That Lucian was endowed with the true spirit of satire, and
a fund of humor rarely possessed by any other writer, is fully
evinced by his works; and, were we to judge from his style,
which was formed upon that of the best models of Greek genius,
we would be led to believe that he flourished in the classic era
of Greek literature.

Plutarch, a native of Cheronea, in Bœotia, was born about
the middle of the first century; the exact period of his birth is
unknown. He commenced his studies when quite young, and,
as he enjoyed the instructions of excellent teachers, he made
rapid progress in the various departments of belles-lettres and
mathematics. At a very early age he was employed by his fellow-citizens in negotiations with the neighboring cities, and this
was subsequently the motive of his visiting Rome, where, when
his public business did not interfere, he gave lectures in philosophy and eloquence. He did not, however, remain at Rome for

any length of time, but returned to his native land, where he was incessantly engaged in the services of his countrymen. The works of Plutarch are very voluminous, but the one for which he is most celebrated is "The Parallel Lives." This contains short biographical notices of forty-four individuals—the most illustrious of the ancient Greeks and Romans—in such a manner that a Greek is always compared with a Roman. Besides these he wrote five isolated biographies, and twelve or fourteen others which are lost. These works are no less interesting than instructive, and for the historian they are invaluable, as they contain many facts which cannot be found in any other history. He is, however, in

PLUTARCH.

these works chargeable with one great defect, viz., an entire neglect of all chronological order—a fault which occasions in the mind of the reader only a confused impression of what he has gone over. Besides these, Plutarch was the author of several other works, some of which were of an historical and others of a philosophical nature; but, as they are comparatively only of minor importance, we shall pass them by without further comment.

St. John Chrysostom.—"The Homily" which St. John pronounced in favor of Eutropius is translated in many colleges, and may surely be considered as a masterpiece of eloquence. However, some passages show bad taste, which we always find in the works of Greek writers who do not belong to the classical period of literature.

Many names might be added, but we had to confine ourselves, as we have said, within the limits of what may be strictly called classical literature.

THE END.

Germania and Agricola of Caius Cornelius Tacitus:

With Notes for Colleges. By W. S. TYLER, Professor of the Greek and Latin Languages in Amherst College. 12mo, 193 pages.

Tacitus's account of Germany and life of Agricola are among the most fascinating and instructive Latin classics. The present edition has been prepared expressly for college classes, by one who knows what they need. In it will be found: 1. A Latin text, approved by all the more recent editors. 2. A copious illustration of the grammatical constructions, as well as of the rhetorical and poetical usages peculiar to Tacitus. In a writer so concise it has been deemed necessary to pay particular regard to the connection of thought, and to the particles as the hinges of that connection. 3. Constant comparisons of the writer with the authors of the Augustan age, for the purpose of indicating the changes which had already been wrought in the language of the Roman people. 4. An embodiment in small compass of the most valuable labors of such recent German critics as Grimm, Günther, Gruber, Kiessling, Dronke, Roth, Ruperti, and Walther.

From PROF. LINCOLN, *of Brown University.*

"I have found the book in daily use with my class of very great service, very practical, and well suited to the wants of students. I am very much pleased with the Life of Tacitus and the Introduction, and indeed with the literary character of the book throughout. We shall make the book a part of our Latin course."

The History of Tacitus:

By W. S. TYLER. With Notes for Colleges. 12mo, 453 pages.

The text of Tacitus is here presented in a form as correct as a comparison of the best editions can make it. Notes are appended for the student's use, which contain not only the grammatical, but likewise all the geographical, archæological, and historical illustrations that are necessary to render the author intelligible. It has been the constant aim of the editor to carry students beyond the dry details of grammar and lexicography, and introduce them to a familiar acquaintance and lively sympathy with the author and his times. Indexes to the notes, and to the names of persons and places, render reference easy.

From PROF. HACKETT, *of Newton Theological Seminary.*

"The notes appear to me to be even more neat and elegant than those on the 'Germania and Agricola.' They come as near to such notes as I would be glad to write myself on a classic, as almost any thing that I have yet seen."

The Works of Horace.

With English Notes, for the use of Schools and Colleges. By J. I. LINCOLN, Professor of the Latin Language and Literature in Brown University. 12mo, 575 pages.

The text of this edition is mainly that of Orelli, the most important readings of other critics being given in foot-notes. The volume is introduced with a biographical sketch of Horace and a critique on his writings, which enable the student to enter intelligently on his work. Peculiar grammatical constructions, as well as geographical and historical allusions, are explained in notes, which are just full enough to aid the pupil, to excite him to gain a thorough understanding of the author, and awaken in him a taste for philological studies, without taking all labor off his hands. While the chief aim has been to impart a clear idea of Latin Syntax as exhibited in the text, it has also been a cherished object to take advantage of the means so variously and richly furnished by Horace for promoting the poetical taste and literary culture of the student.

From an article by PROF. BAHR, *of the University of Heidelberg, in the Heidelberg Annals of Literature.*

"There are already several American editions of Horace, intended for the use of schools; of one of these, which has passed through many editions, and has also been widely circulated in England, mention has been formerly made in this journal; but that one we may not put upon an equality with the one now before us, inasmuch as this has taken a different stand-point, which may serve as a sign of progress in this department of study. The editor has, it is true, also intended his work for the use of schools, and has sought to adapt it, in all its parts, to such a use; but still, without losing sight of this purpose, he has proceeded throughout with more independence. In the preparation of the Notes, the editor has faithfully observed the principles (laid down in his preface); the explanations of the poet's words commend themselves by a compressed brevity which limits itself to what is most essential, and by a sharp precision of expression; and references to other passages of the poet, and also to grammars, dictionaries, etc., are not wanting."

Sallust's Jugurtha and Catiline.

With Notes and a Vocabulary. By NOBLE BUTLER and MINARD STURGIS. 12mo, 897 pages.

The editors have spent a vast amount of time and labor in correcting the text, by a comparison of the most improved German and English editions. It is believed that this will be found superior to any edition hitherto published in this country. In accordance with their chronological order, the "Jugurtha" precedes the "Catiline." The Notes are copious and tersely expressed; they display not only fine scholarship, but (what is quite as necessary in such a book) a practical knowledge of the difficulties which the student encounters in reading this author, and the aids that he requires. The Vocabulary was prepared by the late WILLIAM H. G. BUTLER. It will be found an able and faithful performance.

Virgil's Æneid.

With Explanatory Notes. By HENRY S. FRIEZE, Professor of Latin in the State University of Michigan. Illustrated. 12mo, 598 pages.

The appearance of this edition of Virgil's Æneid will, it is believed, be hailed with delight by all classical teachers. Neither expense nor pains have been spared to clothe the great Latin epic in a fitting dress. The type is unusually large and distinct, and errors in the text, so annoying to the learner, have been carefully avoided. The work contains eighty-five engravings, which delineate the usages, costumes, weapons, arts, and mythology of the ancients with a vividness that can be attained only by pictorial illustrations. The great feature of this edition is the scholarly and judicious commentary furnished in the appended Notes. The author has here endeavored not to show his learning, but to supply such practical aid as will enable the pupil to understand and appreciate what he reads. The notes are just full enough, thoroughly explaining the most difficult passages, while they are not so extended as to take all labor off the pupil's hands. Properly used, they cannot fail to impart an intelligent acquaintance with the syntax of the language. In a word, this work is commended to teachers as the most elegant, accurate, interesting, and practically useful edition of the Æneid that has yet been published.

From JOHN H. BRUNNER, *President of Hiwasse College.*

"The typography, paper, and binding of Virgil's Æneid, by Prof. Frieze, are all that need be desired; while the learned and judicious notes appended, are very valuable indeed."

From Principal of Piedmont (Va.) Academy.

"I have to thank you for a copy of Prof. Frieze's edition of the Æneid. I have been exceedingly pleased in my examination of it. The size of the type from which the text is printed, and the faultless execution, leave nothing to be desired in these respects. The adherence to a standard text throughout, increases the value of this edition."

From D. G. MOORE, *Principal U. High School, Rutland.*

"The copy of Frieze's 'Virgil' forwarded to me was duly received. It is so evidently superior to any of the other editions, that I shall unhesitatingly adopt it in my classes."

Select Orations of M. Tullius Cicero :

With Notes, for the use of Schools and Colleges. By E. A. JOHN-
SON, Professor of Latin in the University of New York. 12mo,
459 pages.

This edition of Cicero's Select Orations possesses some special advantages for the student which are both new and important. It is the only edition which contains the improved text that has been prepared by a recent careful collation and correct deciphering
of the best manuscripts of Cicero's writings. It is the work of the celebrated Orelli, Mad-
vig, and Klotz, and has been done since the appearance of Orelli's complete edition. The
Notes, by Professor Johnson, of the New York University, have been mostly selected,
with great care, from the best German authors, as well as the English edition of Arnold.

From THOMAS CHASE, *Tutor in Latin in Harvard University.*

"An edition of Cicero like Johnson's has long been wanted; and the excellence of the
text, the illustrations of words, particles, and pronouns, and the explanation of various
points of construction and interpretation, bear witness to the Editor's familiarity with
some of the most important results of modern scholarship, and entitle his work to a large
share of public favor."

"It seems to us an improvement upon any edition of these Orations that has been
published in this country, and will be found a valuable aid in their studies to the lovers
of classical literature."—*Troy Daily Whig.*

Cicero de Officiis :

With English Notes, mostly translated from ZUMPT and BONNELL. By
THOMAS A. THACHER, of Yale College. 12mo, 194 pages.

In this edition, a few historical notes have been introduced in cases where the Dictionary in common use has not been found to contain the desired information; the design
of which is to aid the learner in understanding the contents of the treatises, the thoughts
and reasoning of the author, to explain grammatical difficulties, and inculcate a knowledge of grammatical principles. The Editor has aimed throughout to guide rather than
carry the learner through difficulties; requiring of him more study, in consequence of
his help, than he would have devoted to the book without it.

From M. L. STOEVER, *Professor of the Latin Language and Literature in Pennsyl-
vania College.*

"I have examined with much pleasure Prof. Thacher's edition of Cicero de Officiis,
and am convinced of its excellence. The Notes have been prepared with great care and
good judgment. Practical knowledge of the wants of the student has enabled the Editor
to furnish just the kind of assistance required; grammatical difficulties are removed, and
the obscurities of the treatise are explained, the interest of the learner is elicited, and his
industry directed rather than superseded. There can be but one opinion with regard to
the merits of the work, and I trust that Professor Thacher will be disposed to continue
his labors so carefully commenced, in this department of classical learning."

Lincoln's Livy.

Selections from the first Five Books, together with the Twenty-First and Twenty-Second Books entire; with a Plan of Rome, a Map of the passage of Hannibal, and English Notes for the use of Schools. By J. L. LINCOLN, Professor of the Latin Language and Literature in Brown University. 12mo, 329 pages.

The publishers believe that in this edition of Livy a want is supplied which has been universally felt; there being previous to this no American edition furnished with the requisite aids for the successful study of this Latin author. The text is chiefly that of Alschefski, which is now generally received by the best critics. The notes have been prepared with special reference to the grammatical study of the language, and the illustration of its forms, constructions, and idioms, as used by Livy. They will not be found to foster habits of dependence in the student, by supplying indiscriminate translation or unnecessary assistance; but come to his help only in such parts as it is fair to suppose he cannot master by his own exertions. They also embrace all necessary information relating to history, geography, and antiquities.

Lincoln's Livy has been highly commended by critics, and is used in nearly all the colleges in the country.

From Prof. Anderson, *of Waterville College.*

"A careful examination of several portions of your work has convinced me that, for the use of students, it is altogether superior to any edition of Livy with which I am acquainted. Among its excellences you will permit me to name the close attention given to particles, to the subjunctive mood, the constant reference to the grammars, the discrimination of words nearly synonymous, and the care in giving the localities mentioned in the text. The book will be hereafter used in our college."

Beza's Latin Version of the New Testament.

12mo, 291 pages.

The now-acknowledged propriety of giving students of languages familiar works for translation—thus adopting in the schools the mode by which the child first learns to talk —has induced the publication of this new American edition of Beza's Latin Version of the New Testament. Ever since its first appearance, this work has kept its place in the general esteem; while more recent versions have been so strongly tinged with the peculiar views of the translators as to make them acceptable to particular classes only. The editor has exerted himself to render the present edition worthy of patronage by its superior accuracy and neatness; and the publishers flatter themselves that the pains bestowed will insure for it a preference over other editions.

Cæsar's Commentaries on the Gallic War.

With English Notes, Critical and Explanatory; a Lexicon, Geographical and Historical Indexes, a Map of Gaul, etc. By Rev. J. A. SPENCER, D. D. 12mo, 408 pages.

In the preparation of this volume, great care has been taken to adapt it in every respect to the wants of the young student, to make it a means at the same time of advancing him in a thorough knowledge of Latin, and inspiring him with a desire for further acquaintance with the classics of the language. Dr. Spencer has not, like some commentators, given an abundance of help on the easy passages, and allowed the difficult ones to speak for themselves. His Notes are on those parts on which the pupil wants them, and explain, not only grammatical difficulties, but allusions of every kind in the text. A well-drawn sketch of Cæsar's life, a Map of the region in which his campaigns were carried on, and a Vocabulary, which removes the necessity of using a large dictionary and the waste of time consequent thereon, enhance the value of the volume in no small degree.

Quintus Curtius:

Life and Exploits of Alexander the Great. Edited and illustrated with English Notes. By WILLIAM HENRY CROSBY. 12mo, 385 pages.

Curtius's History of Alexander the Great, though little used in the schools of this country, in England and on the Continent holds a high place in the estimation of classical instructors. The interesting character of its subject, the elegance of its style, and the purity of its moral sentiments, ought to place it at least on a par with Cæsar's Commentaries or Sallust's Histories. The present edition, by the late Professor of Latin in Rutgers College, is unexceptionable in typography, convenient in form, scholarly and practical in its notes, and altogether an admirable text-book for classes preparing for college.

From PROF. OWEN, of the New York Free Academy.

"It gives me great pleasure to add my testimonial to the many you are receiving in favor of the beautiful and well-edited edition of Quintus Curtius, by Prof. Wm. Henry Crosby. It is seldom that a classical book is submitted to me for examination, to which I can give so hearty a recommendation as to this. The external appearance is attractive; the paper, type, and binding, being just what a text-book should be, neat, clear, and durable. The notes are brief, pertinent, scholar-like, neither too exuberant nor too meagre, but happily exemplifying the golden mean so desirable and yet so very difficult of attainment."

A Latin Grammar for Schools and Colleges.

By A. HARKNESS, Ph. D., Professor in Brown University.

To explain the general plan of the work, the Publishers ask the attention of teachers to the following extracts from the Preface:

1. This volume is designed to present a systematic arrangement of the great facts and laws of the Latin language; to exhibit not only grammatical forms and constructions, but also those *vital principles* which underlie, control, and explain them.

2. Designed at once as a text-book for the class-room, and a book of reference in study, it aims to introduce the beginner easily and pleasantly to the first principles of the language, and yet to make adequate provision for the wants of the more advanced student.

3. By brevity and conciseness in the choice of phraseology and compactness in the arrangement of forms and topics, the author has endeavored to compress within the limits of a convenient manual an amount of carefully-selected grammatical facts, which would otherwise fill a much larger volume.

4. He has, moreover, endeavored to present the whole subject in the light of modern scholarship. Without encumbering his pages with any unnecessary discussions, he has aimed to enrich them with the *practical results* of the recent labors in the field of philology.

5. Syntax has received in every part special attention. An attempt has been made to exhibit, as clearly as possible, that beautiful system of laws which the genius of the language—that highest of all grammatical authority—has created for itself.

6. Topics which require extended illustration are first presented in their completeness in general outline, before the separate points are discussed in detail. Thus a single page often foreshadows all the leading features of an extended discussion, imparting a completeness and vividness to the impression of the learner, impossible under any other treatment.

7. Special care has been taken to explain and illustrate with the requisite fulness all difficult and intricate subjects. The Subjunctive Mood—that severest trial of the teacher's patience—has been presented, it is hoped, in a form at once simple and comprehensive.

Arnold's Greek Course.

Revised, Corrected, and Improved, by the Rev. J. A. SPENCER, D. D., late Professor of Latin and Oriental Languages in Burlington College, N. J.

FIRST GREEK BOOK, on the Plan of the First Latin Book. 12mo, 254 pages.

PRACTICAL INTRODUCTION TO GREEK PROSE COMPOSITION. 12mo, 237 pages.

SECOND PART TO THE ABOVE. 12mo, 248 pages.

GREEK READING BOOK. Containing the substance of the Practical Introduction to Greek Construing, and a Treatise on the Greek Particles; also, copious selections from Greek Authors, with Critical and Explanatory English Notes, and a Lexicon. 12mo, 618 pages.

A complete, thorough, practical, and easy Greek course is here presented. The beginner commences with the " First Book," in which the elementary principles of the language are unfolded, not in abstract language, difficult both to comprehend and to remember, but as practically applied in sentences. Throughout the whole, the pupil sees just where he stands, and is taught to use and apply what he learns. His progress is, therefore, as rapid as it is intelligent and pleasant. There is no unnecessary verbiage, nor is the pupil's attention diverted from what is really important by a mass of minor details. It is the experience of teachers who use this book, that with it a given amount of Greek Grammar can be imparted to a pupil in a shorter time and with far less trouble than with any other text-book.

The " First Book " may with advantage be followed by the " Introduction to Greek Prose Composition." The object of this work is to enable the student, as soon as he can decline and conjugate with tolerable facility, to translate simple sentences after given examples and with given words; the principles employed being those of imitation and very frequent repetition. It is at once a Syntax, a Vocabulary, and an Exercise-book. The " Second Part " carries the subject further, unfolding the most complicated constructions, and the nicest points of Latin Syntax. A Key is provided for the teacher's use.

The " Reader," besides extracts judiciously selected from the Greek classics, contains valuable instructions to guide the learner in translating and construing, and a complete exposition of the particles, their signification and government. It is a fitting sequel to the earlier parts of the course, everywhere showing the hand of an acute critic, an accomplished scholar, and an experienced teacher.

From the REV. DR. COLEMAN, *Professor of Greek and Latin, Princeton, N. J.*

" I can, from the most satisfactory experience, bear testimony to the excellence of your series of Text-Books for Schools. I am in the daily use of Arnold's Latin and Greek Exercises, and consider them decidedly superior to any other Elementary Works in those languages. '

www.ingramcontent.com/pod-product-compliance
Lightning Source LLC
Chambersburg PA
CBHW030111030726
47498CB00007B/2333